One Small Candle

Mayflower and the Pilgrim Fathers

Philip Quenby

O&U
Onwards & Upwards

Onwards and Upwards Publishers

4 The Old Smithy, London Road, Rockbeare,
EX5 2EA, United Kingdom.
www.onwardsandupwards.org

First edition, published in the United Kingdom by Onwards and Upwards Publishers (2021).

ISBN: 978-1-78815-749-0
Typeface: Sabon LT

About the Author

Writer and film-maker Philip Quenby, formerly a partner in an international law firm, has a passion for understanding what the past has to say to us today.

His first book, *Redeeming A Nation*, offered biblical reflections on over a thousand years of English history, whilst the follow-up *One Small Candle* uses the story of the Mayflower Pilgrims to emphasise the importance of a biblical worldview for the development of freedom, democracy and rule of law.

His five-part documentary *Magna Carta Unlocked*[1] examines how and why modern civil liberties grew on the back of a failed peace treaty – and what part the Bible played in that process.

To contact the author, please write to:

Philip Quenby
c/o Onwards and Upwards Publishers Ltd.
4 The Old Smithy
London Road
Rockbeare
EX5 2EA

More information about the author can be found on the book's web page:

www.onwardsandupwards.org/one-small-candle

---

[1] See *magnacartaunlocked.com*

"Thus out of small beginnings, greater things have been produced by His hand that made all things of nothing, and gives being to all things that are; and, as one small candle may light a thousand, so the light here kindled hath shone unto many, yea in some sort to our whole nation; let the glorious name of Jehovah have all the praise."

William Bradford
Governor of Plymouth Plantation

Contents

Foreword

AS A MEMBER OF THE PILGRIMS' SOCIETY, I AM DELIGHTED TO
introduce this book. Four centuries may have passed since the Pilgrim Fathers
sailed for America in September 1620, but what they represent is as important –
and as fought over – now as it has ever been. Malcolm X once said, "I didn't land
on Plymouth Rock, Plymouth Rock landed on me," and that sentiment is still
being expressed today. But if we are to find the right balance between (on the one
hand) rejecting out of hand everything about the Pilgrims simply because we do
not share their views or like everything they did and (on the other hand) endorsing
each and all their actions for no better reason than blind loyalty, we need to be
able to put them and their ideas in context. This book does precisely that. In doing
so, it goes to the heart of the main issues of their time and ours: the choice between
freedom or dictatorship, between law as merely the say-so of whoever happens to
be in power or as something we cannot simply change to suit ourselves, between
government as little more than the imposition of brute force or as being rooted in
the consent of the governed.

This is a short book, written in a way anyone can understand, but the ideas it
contains are profound. There is much in it that was new to me and, I suspect, will
be new to most readers, too. It illuminates the divide at the heart of United States'
society – a divide replicated in Western culture as a whole. The Pilgrim Fathers
and those who followed later to help build Puritan New England saw America as
a "city on a hill", a nation self-consciously rooted in the Christian faith, with a
mission to spread light to the world; whereas the Founding Fathers, though
acknowledging it was "self-evident" that all human beings had been "endowed by
their Creator" with various attributes and rights, owed a debt to the thinking of
Jean-Jacques Rousseau and the Enlightenment that pulled in a different direction.
A tug of war between these twin inheritances lies behind much of our present-day
culture wars, and hence the need for us to get to grips with where these competing
ideologies lead. The inheritance we claim to value so highly – freedom, democracy,
rule of law and more – was forged in religious persecution and has only been kept
alive through the willingness of past generations to fight in its defence. The jury is
out as to whether we will show as much resolve on that score as our forefathers.
We certainly will not be able to do so unless we understand what is at stake, and
why.

Sometimes we need the help of the past to illuminate the present. At a time of
confusion about our values and freedoms – where they come from, whether they
are worthwhile, even what they are – there could scarcely be a better time to go

back and reflect on original sources. This is the story of the Pilgrims, but it is also our story.

Simon Reading
Marquis of Reading

Preface

MY FRIEND PHILIP QUENBY HAS GALVANISED THE IMPORTANCE OF remembering the stories of our historic roots, which are so very important to our heritage. These beginnings must never be forgotten and need to be passed down through the generations with understanding of our foundations. We must never remove the ancient landmarks and should walk in their ways once again to maintain this rich inheritance which has been passed to us all! Against all odds, facing a storm-tossed angry sea, under dire circumstances in the middle of a cold winter, facing a sure death either by freezing or starvation, the providential hand of God led and provided by faith for a people who honoured His name. The name above all names. John Robinson, the Pilgrims' pastor, was my great grandfather from ten generations and four hundred years ago. Therefore, I am humbled and eternally grateful for that bloodline. May we fulfil the great commission of preaching the Gospel of the Kingdom prior to our King's return.

The Pilgrims: A Model of Christian Character

The Separatist Movement began in England in the latter part of the 16th century, as people began to embrace the idea of "reformation without tarrying for any". The many Separatists in and around the little town of Scrooby in the north of England were destined to have a great impact upon the world, for it was here that many of the Pilgrims had their roots. At Scrooby, these Christians wrote a church covenant – the first of its kind affirming church self-government – in 1606.

Three of the most prominent leaders of the Pilgrims started on their great pilgrimage from Scrooby. As we briefly look at their lives, we will begin to understand the heart of the Pilgrims.

WILLIAM BREWSTER

William Brewster was one of the only Pilgrims to have a position in English society, and that was by no means an exalted one. After serving as a confidential secretary to a prominent member of Queen Elizabeth's court, he returned to Scrooby where he became Postmaster and the overseer of a gentleman's estate in the area. "He set about trying to reform the Church of England from within by getting good scriptural preachers for the local churches and paying for them out of his own pocket. (Many churches went without preaching for years on end, since Queen Elizabeth plainly preferred the reading of government-approved 'homilies' to sermons that reflected individual interpretation of Scripture.) When the Church of England demanded more rigid conformity to its rituals and rejected the right of individuals to hear 'unauthorized' preachers, Brewster finally decided to separate from the Church and to covenant with other Christians in his area to form a scriptural congregation."

Brewster later served as an elder in the congregation in England, Holland and America. During the first year in America, the Pilgrims had no pastor, so Brewster effectively served in that capacity. According to Bradford, he was also a highly effective evangelist – "He did more in this behalf in a year than many ... do in all their lives."

JOHN ROBINSON

It is written that more than anyone else, John Robinson prepared the Pilgrims to accomplish the great task of preparing the way for the settlement of a new nation. It was he who served as the Pilgrims' pastor in England and Holland.

Robinson was trained as a clergyman in the Church of England, but was "dismissed from his first pastoral assignment for failure to conform to the Church of England's requirements regarding the wearing of priestly vestments". Afterwards he took much time in considering whether he should remain in the Church of England. While he witnessed much that was unscriptural in the Church, he hesitated, for there were many godly men who still remained in the Church. Yet the truth of God burned in his heart. Robinson said, "...had not the truth been in my heart as a burning fire shut up in my bones ... wherein I was straitly tied, but had suffered the light of God to have been put out in mine own unthankful heart by other men's darkness."

The truth did prevail, and the light within him burned brighter as he left the Church of England and joined the Separatist congregation that met in the home of William Brewster in Scrooby.

Marshall Foster says that "[t]hough often neglected by historians, John Robinson should be known as one of the great Christian philosophers who propounded religious toleration in an intolerant age and representative government in an age of absolute monarchy. For twenty years, he taught these principles in depth to his persecuted and beloved Pilgrim church. More than any other man, John Robinson prepared a people to take dominion over the wilderness to the glory of God. Through his godly wisdom, he taught the Pilgrims individual Christian unity.

"His love was great towards them, and his care was all ways bent for their best good, both for soul and body; for besides his singular abilities in divine things (wherein he excelled), he was also very able to give directions in civil affairs, and to foresee dangers and inconveniences; by which means he was very helpful to their outward estates, and so was every way as a common father unto them..."

WILLIAM BRADFORD

One of the best-known Pilgrim Fathers was William Bradford. He served as governor of Plymouth for 33 years and also wrote the History of Plymouth Plantation, the first great literary work of America.

As a young teenager, Bradford reasoned that the Church of England was unbiblical and so removed himself from it. He had such an insight because a few years earlier, while confined to bed with a long illness, he had read the Bible continuously. He attended the Church of England in Bobworth for some time simply because he was impressed by the scriptural preaching of Rev. Richard Clyfton. When Clyfton withdrew and joined the Scrooby Congregation, Bradford followed, even though he faced enormous pressure. He decided "to withdraw from the communion of the parish-assemblies, and engage with some society of the faithful that should keep close unto the written word of God, as the rule of their worship ... although the provoked rage of his friends tried all the ways imaginable to reclaim him from it, unto all ... his answer was ... 'Nevertheless, to keep a good conscience, and walk in such a way as God has prescribed in his word, is a thing which I must prefer before you all, and above life itself.'"

It was 1602 when Bradford started attending the Separatist Church in Scrooby. Six years later he would travel with part of the Church to Holland, and twelve years after that with a smaller number to America.

Kevin Jessip
Global Strategic Alliance

One Small Candle

Introduction

WHY DOES THE STORY OF THE MAYFLOWER PILGRIMS STILL MATTER and what can justify another book about them? There is no shortage of material – much of it excellent – to supplement what they and their contemporaries have bequeathed us.

To put it another way: what special claim do these people have on our attention? What makes them different from settlers in Jamestown, Virginia (or any other English colony in the New World, for that matter)? They were few in number, they were not powerful or significant individuals in the way the world reckons these things, and they were hardly much missed at home. The people we call Pilgrim Fathers were a minority within a minority – easy to dismiss (then and now) as cranks, troublemakers or fanatics.

The answer is: an idea, a book and an inheritance. The idea was freedom – specifically, freedom of conscience – the book was the Geneva Bible and the inheritance was the accumulation of English liberties bound up in all that *Magna Carta* has come to symbolise. With freedom of conscience more and more under threat at home and abroad, remembering how and why our forefathers stood firm against overbearing state power is not just topical, but vital.

This book investigates the ideas and motivations that brought the Pilgrims to the New World, setting them alongside King James' contrasting autocratic vision for church and state. Parallels with today will be readily apparent.

We sometimes arrogantly assume the denizens of a more religious age to be ignorant, uneducated and credulous, too seldom pausing to observe how their reflex pieties have equivalents in our own thinking. In truth, people in the 17th century were no more stupid or gullible than we are. They acted within different parameters, undoubtedly, but were no less intelligent or rational. They deserve a fair hearing in the court of modern opinion.

Which brings us to Thanksgiving and what the Pilgrims' story has to say to us today. Celebrating their legacy does not (should not) mean turning a blind eye to injustice, wrongdoing and human failings. But neither does it mean we should ignore what is good. As we look back on four centuries since the *Mayflower* sailed and her passengers disembarked to start a new life in a strange land, we could do worse than begin by recalling the words of their Governor, William Bradford:

> "Yea, let them which have been redeemed of the Lord, shew how He hath delivered them from the hand of the oppressor. When they wandered in the desert wilderness out of the way, and found no city to dwell in, both hungry and thirsty, their soul was overwhelmed in

them. Let them confess before the Lord His loving kindness and His wonderful works before the sons of men."

If ever there was a time when we need historical perspective, this is surely it. Beset by trials of many kinds, seemingly hemmed in before and behind, too often we give the impression of groping blindly in the dark instead of seeking answers where they might readily be found. The Mayflower Pilgrims' experiences offer three things currently in short supply: hope, purpose and direction.

Hope, because no-one in the early 1600s could possibly have envisaged what would come out of the sufferings, struggles and even the apparent setbacks of a small group of comparative nobodies. Their endeavours were marked at every stage by what looked like failure – driven from their homeland by the repression of a king to form an embattled immigrant community in Europe, even in America they signally failed to create the godly society they craved. Yet despite all that, they laid foundations for what became the mightiest and wealthiest nation the world has ever seen. If this could be true of them, there is no reason why it cannot be true for us, too. As one of ancient Israel's prophets put it, "Who despises the day of small things?" (Zechariah 4:10).

Purpose, because (despite what we may think) each of us has significance. The Pilgrims operated in a political environment where they were weak and powerless, but they did not allow that to constrain or define them. They believed that all they did and said was important not just for this world, but for the next, and they behaved accordingly. There is nothing to stop us doing likewise.

Direction, because though we have wandered from the right track in the past, we have nevertheless been able to find our way back to firmer ground. Our future trajectory, whether as individuals or as societies, is an issue of choice, and choices made in former years offer guidance for the present. The Bible advises us to, "Stand at the crossroads and look; ask for the ancient paths, ask where the good way is, and walk in it, and you will find rest for your souls." (Jeremiah 6:16).

May we be encouraged, edified and emboldened in our own time of testing as we ponder the lives of those who faced far worse and did not falter.

1

A World on Fire

"1618: In the month of September a terrible comet in the form of a large star with a lengthy whip or tail was visible for a long time. All Christendom suffered its effects for the next 30 years."

Parish record book
Pfungstadt, Germany

CLIMATE CHANGE, RAPID TECHnological innovation, an information revolution, religious and ideological conflict, economic migration, asylum seeking, state attempts to constrain freedom of conscience, empires pitted against emerging nation states... On the surface, the 17th century may look and sound alien with its unfamiliar clothes, habits, language and manners. But appearances are deceptive, for their problems were surprisingly modern. This is an age we need to study and learn from.

The Comets of 1618

Three comets were seen in 1618, widely interpreted as harbingers of misfortune. Even before they appeared, famous mathematician Johannes Kepler had written in his *Astrological Almanac* for the coming year that a conjunction of five planets in May would see extreme climatic events, warning that if a comet came, too, people ought to "sharpen their pens" – meaning that war and upheavals would soon follow. Learned men disputed whether comets were atmospheric anomalies, optical illusions or genuine heavenly bodies moving among the planets, but few doubted they boded ill.

Climate Change

Decreased sunspot activity during the 17th century (observed using newly developed refracting telescopes) reduced the amount of solar energy reaching earth, making temperatures fall. Winters grew longer and harsher, summers cooler and wetter. More than once contemporaries spoke of a "year without a summer". Harvests failed, bringing malnutrition, disease, civil disorder and war. In 1617-18 there were almost no sunspots, and very few during 1625-26 and 1637-39. Today there are more sunspots in a single year than appeared in the seven decades from 1643-1715.

If there is one thing we think we know about the Mayflower Pilgrims, it is that they were fleeing religious persecution. That is true, but of course there was much more to it than that. Conflict over religion was not a sideshow or bigotry for the mere sake of it. Religion was at the heart of the main political and social issues of the day. To understand the Pilgrims and to understand ourselves, we need to see why – and how the ideas these refugees took from the Bible and from their mother country helped create the modern world.

Societies throughout the 1600s were under pressure – from falling temperatures and the famine and disease that came in their wake, from new ideas and novel ways of communicating them, from war, economic dislocation and natural disasters, from popular resistance to state attempts at enforcing conformity, from changing expectations on the part

---

Religious Strife

France's Wars of Religion between Catholics and Protestants (the Huguenots) caused an estimated 3 million deaths in the three decades before 1598, when the Edict of Nantes granted limited toleration towards Huguenots. The Eighty Years' War (Dutch Revolt) of 1568-1648 similarly took on a sectarian flavour, with atrocities like the "Spanish Fury" at Maastricht in 1579, when all but 400 out of a town numbering 30,000 were massacred. But the Thirty Years' War (1618-48) brought the worst death toll of all, with possibly as much as a third of the population of Germany perishing.

---

of their citizens. Adding ideological conflict to this mix was like putting a match to tinder. This was the Pilgrims' world – an often-frightening place where old certainties were being challenged at every turn. Responses by governments varied, driven by practical necessity but also by ideology. Nowhere did people act blindly, for they were no more foolish or credulous than we are.

All cultures have a dominant ideology. In Europe at this point that meant Christianity, but the former cohesion of Western Christendom had been shattered by the Protestant Reformation – unleashed by the publication in 1517 of Martin Luther's 95 theses criticising church corruption and false doctrine. This split the religious

---

The Thirty Years' War

In 1618 a Protestant uprising in Bohemia against the rule of Holy Roman Emperor Ferdinand II (an Austrian Hapsburg and a Catholic) ignited sectarian conflict throughout Germany and increasingly drew in foreign powers – Spain, Denmark, Sweden, Poland, France. English king James Stuart kept aloof, despite his daughter Elizabeth briefly being Queen of Bohemia after her husband Frederick V, Elector Palatine was persuaded by the rebels to accept the throne. It proved a disastrous decision, as Imperial forces soon chased the couple from their new realm and overran the Palatinate, too.

---

landscape between, on the one hand, Roman Catholics who remained loyal to the Pope and traditional church teaching and, on the other, reformers who recognised the Bible as their only authority and rejected the old hierarchy. The resulting upheaval shook entire nations to the core, with repercussions as profound for politics as for religion. Alliances and loyalties were in flux, raising the spectre of new enemies abroad and a potential fifth column at home – this threat felt especially keenly

---

The Ottoman Empire

Europe was threatened from outside as well as tearing itself apart from within. Despite Hapsburg-led victory over the Ottoman Turks' navy at Lepanto in 1571, Christendom seldom presented a united front against Muslim raiding and expansionism. Facing only fragmented opposition in the Balkans, in 1605 the Ottomans retook the Hungarian fortresses of Veszprém, Visegrad and Gran, following up in 1620 with a crushing victory over the Poles at the battle of Cecora on the River Prut. The high-water mark of Ottoman power in Europe was not reached until their failure at the siege of Vienna in 1683.

> **Printing**
>
> Though the Chinese had long used printing, Gutenberg's moveable-type press in Mainz, Germany (set up around 1450) brought together several existing technologies – the Roman wine press, the goldsmith's punch, impressionable paper – in a new way. Within decades, presses were operating in Basel, Switzerland (1466), Rome, Italy (1467), Pilsen, Bohemia (1468), Paris, France (1470), London, England (1476) and elsewhere. Both church and secular authorities sporadically tried censorship, but this was seldom entirely effective.

in England, whose Roman Catholic minority were viewed as agents for imperial Spain, the military superpower of the day. Memories of the 1588 Spanish Armada were still fresh and the possibility of attack from outside or rebellion within seemed ever-present. What looks, at times, like government paranoia has to be seen in that context.

Fuelling breakneck change were two processes which fed off each other: moveable type printing and growing

literacy. Pamphlets spread the ideas of Luther and other reformers, whilst printing enabled Bibles to be produced cheaply and in large numbers, freely traded or smuggled into wherever there was a market. This made a practical reality of the Protestant imperative that everyone should have access to the Word of God in their own language. In turn, Scripture available in the vernacular drove an upsurge in the desire to learn to read. Once these twin genies were out of the bottle, they could not

> **The Bible in English**
>
> John Wycliffe produced a translation of the Bible into Middle English in the late 14th century, but by the time William Tyndale began work on a new English translation a century and a half later changes in language had made Wycliffe's Bible almost incomprehensible. Since Henry VIII took a dim view of Scripture being put in the hands of laymen, Tyndale was forced to spend much of his life in hiding on the Continent. Tracked down by an English agent (probably sent by Henry VIII's Lord Chancellor Sir Thomas More), he was strangled and burnt at the stake as a heretic in Brussels in 1536.

be put back in. We have in a very real sense been living with the consequences ever since – the ideas unleashed by reformers and their reading of Scripture forming constant eddies and currents through England's Civil War of the 1640s and subsequent experiment with republican government, America's War of Independence of 1775-1783 and much of what has happened afterwards – issues of freedom, choice, authority, law and consent. These fundamentals are for every time and place, but England in the 1600s threw them into particularly stark relief.

2

Collision Course

"Consider, I am here. I am king. I may demand of you when and what I will."

James Stuart

ENGLAND IN THE FIRST DECADE of the new century was adjusting to foreign rule – by James Stuart, the Scottish king. Coming to power in a bloodless transition in 1603 after Elizabeth I died childless, he was a complex and troubled personality. His father Lord Darnley had been murdered, his mother Mary, Queen of Scots beheaded; two of the regents appointed following her death were respectively assassinated and executed; as a child he had briefly been kidnapped and imprisoned; his education was farmed out to a man who regularly beat him. Physically unimpressive and often coarse in both speech and behaviour, he was also proud and prickly. This was a man keen to display his undoubted learning, to bely suggestions of sympathy with his mother's Catholicism, who personally supervised the torture of women accused of witchcraft. Often depicted as the evil genius behind the Pilgrims' exile and eventual departure for America, he brought with him a view of kingship that was at odds both with traditional English practice and with what Protestant reformers understood the Bible to say. The scene was set for an epic clash of worldviews.

Plots

Both sides of the religious divide sought to exploit confusion following the death of Elizabeth I – the Bye Plot aimed to seize James Stuart and force him to make concessions to Catholics whilst the Main Plot sought to replace him with his English-born cousin Arbella Stuart. Both were quickly discovered, the latter because Arbella Stuart herself reported it. One of those implicated was Sir Walter Raleigh, imprisoned for 13 years in the Tower of London where, in an ironic twist, he was some years later joined by Arbella after she incurred King James' disapproval for marrying without royal permission.

The Millenary Petition

Puritans initially had great hopes of support from the avowedly Protestant James Stuart, and as the king was progressing south in 1603 to take up the English throne, he was presented with a petition allegedly signed by 1,000 Puritan clergymen. This "Millenary Petition" sought abolition of religious practices Puritans considered superstitious and unscriptural, such as confirmation, wedding rings, making the sign of the cross during baptism and bowing at the name of Jesus. In response to it, James convened the Hampton Court conference.

Royal angst was not helped by a succession of conspiracies against the new ruler. The Gunpowder Plot of 1605 (aiming to blow up the king and Parliament so as to put a Catholic on the throne) is the most famous, but there were others. And though England was wealthy and fertile compared with James' Scottish domains, in terms of wider geopolitics she was an economic and military minnow. Her population of about 4 million was dwarfed by France (upwards of 15 million) and the

---

Rival Powers

Government revenues show how far behind her competitors England was. In 1600 revenue from the Spanish empire totalled 15.3 million Venetian ducats. Comparable figures for France were 5.5 million ducats, for the Ottoman Empire 4 million ducats, for Venice and Portugal 2 million ducats apiece, for the United Provinces of the Netherlands 1.1 million ducats, for England 0.9 million ducats, for Poland 0.5 million ducats. South America was the jewel in Spain's crown. When Dutch admiral Piet Heyn surprised a Spanish treasure fleet off Cuba in 1628, he captured 4 million ducats of gold and silver.

Ottoman Empire (in excess of 27 million), let alone imperial Spain's vast dominions and endless supply of loot from South America. She had no standing army, whereas the Spanish infantry were widely reckoned the finest troops in Europe and in terms of sea-power the Dutch were far ahead. Moreover, she was a newcomer to the scramble for overseas possessions, for whilst her zone of control in Ireland was expanding, otherwise she could boast only the merest toehold at Jamestown in Virginia.

Divine Right of Kings

Episcopacy suited King James' view of kingship, whereas he said, "Presbyterianism con-sorteth with monarchy as well as God with the Devil." In *The True Law of Free Monarchies*, James asserted that only "lineal succession" (i.e. birthright) gave a legitimate claim to the crown, a king being "heritable overlord by birth only, and not by any right given in the coronation" (meaning kingly status did not derive from election or consent of the people). There were convenient parallels between this lineal succession and the apostolic succession that bishops claimed through St Peter, reputedly first Bishop of Rome.

For James there were a number of imperatives: to knit his territories into a unified and unitary state; to impose a religious settlement that would bring order and stability in place of the chaos of recent years; to cement royal power in the face of upstart claims from Parliament; to avoid European wars that he had neither the manpower nor the money to fight and win. Informing and overarching all he did and said was his political philosophy – Divine Right of kings, the idea that rulers were

---

The Hampton Court Conference

Held over three days in January 1604, the Hampton Court conference saw the king and anti-Puritan Bishop Richard Bancroft reject all Puritan demands. To add insult to injury, just two months later James made Bancroft Archbishop of Canterbury. Bancroft then presided over production of the King James Bible, a project suggested at the Hampton Court conference which James adopted as a chance to do away with unwelcome commentaries like those in the Geneva Bible – additions the king dismissed as "very partial, untrue, seditious and savouring too much of dangerous and traitorous conceits".

---

appointed by God and were answerable to Him alone. This challenged an English understanding of kingship that had held for hundreds of years, for *Magna Carta*

Delusions of Grandeur

In 1618 King James had the dilapidated Aldersgate entrance to the City of London rebuilt with an arch featuring a statue of himself on horseback. This was flanked by carvings of the Old Testament prophets Samuel and Jeremiah and underneath these the quotation: "Then shall enter the gates of this city kings and princes sitting on the throne of David, riding on chariots and horses, they and their princes accompanied by the men of Judah and the inhabitants of Jerusalem; and this city shall remain forever." (Jeremiah 17:25)

---

emphatically stated that no monarch was above the law. Now James said precisely the opposite. The disastrous logic of these irreconcilable positions was fully played out after his death, as heavy-handed application of Divine Right's principles by his son and successor Charles I drove the country to civil war. For now, Parliament grumbled and the nation grew restive, but there was still peace.

Peace, that is, unless you were on the receiving end of government policies towards dissenters and religious minorities. Penalties were applied to Roman Catholics but also to those at the opposite end of the religious spectrum. Hierarchy and top-down control in the church were important politically because they buttressed a monarchy that rested on the same principles – as James himself pithily observed, "No bishops, no king." The semi-reformed Church of England looked like a perfect vehicle for state control, organised around bishops and archbishops with the king at its head and the *Prayer Book* as a medium for ensuring conformity. So old laws were enforced more stringently or new ones put in place to make sure that

---

King of Great Britain

As king of Scotland, England, Wales and (nominally, at least) Ireland, James liked to style himself King of Great Britain. Fancying himself a Bible scholar, he had a gold coin struck – the Jacobus – bearing in Latin a prophecy from the Old Testament book of Ezekiel: "I will make of them one nation in the land on the mountains of Israel; and one king shall be over them all; they shall no longer be two nations, nor shall they ever be divided into two kingdoms again." (Ezekiel 37:22). In fact, despite sharing the same monarch, Scotland and England remained quite distinct politically and legally.

---

attendance at this church was rigorously policed, backed up by fines and imprisonment. (Again, the logical conclusions of compulsory uniformity were seen a generation later when Charles I tried to impose a Prayer Book on Presbyterian Scotland, the resulting uproar eventually consuming not only the territories which owed him allegiance but even the king himself, beheaded in 1649 for crimes against his own people.)

3

Fuel to the Flames

"The people shall not be excused, when they do evil at the commandment of their governors."

The Geneva Bible

NO LONGER HAVING PAPAL authority as a counterweight to royal despotism, English Protestants sought guidance from the Bible on how to react as James unfolded his vision for church and state. From the religious perspective, his policies were unwelcome both to Puritans, who aimed to purify the Church of England of all remaining Catholic influences, and to Separatists, who shunned an institution they saw as irredeemably corrupt and wanted freedom to go their own way.

Puritans and Separatists

In *Shaping History through Prayer and Fasting* the respected Bible teacher Derek Prince observes, "The difference between Puritans and Pilgrims could be expressed in the two words Reformation and Restoration. Puritans sought to reform the church as it existed in their day. The pilgrims believed that the ultimate purpose of God was to restore the church to its original condition, as portrayed in the New Testament." Hence William Bradford's yearning that "the churches of God revert to their ancient purity and recover their primitive [i.e. original] order, liberty and beauty".

Instead of working to reform the established church from within, like Puritans, Separatists withdrew from an ungodly world to seek holiness on their own terms.

Shakespeare

Characters in *Twelfth Night* (written in 1601, two years before James Stuart came to the English throne) poke fun at both Puritans and Separatists. Hearing pantomime villain Malvolio likened to a Puritan, Sir Andrew Aguecheek exclaims, "If I thought that, I'd beat him like a dog" (Act II scene iii), later saying, "I'd as lief be a Brownist as a politician" (Act III scene ii). Brownist was another name for Separatist – a reference to Robert Browne, an early exponent of Separatist views. Malvolio was probably modelled on a well-known Elizabethan Puritan, courtier William Knollys.

They did so in illegal religious gatherings under leaders they chose for themselves. Here they read the Bible, sang Psalms and "prophesied", with each in turn standing to discuss Scripture as they earnestly sought God's will. The mass participation, spontaneity and sheer passion of these meetings contrasted sharply with state-approved churches where appointed clergy followed a set liturgy, making congregations often seem little more than spectators.

Just as there could be no compromise between *Magna Carta* and Divine Right of kings, so there was no common ground between Separatists and government edicts on church affairs. These religious radicals offered no threat of armed insurrection, did not aim at political revolution and wanted only to live quietly in pursuit of what they saw as true Christianity, but nevertheless they were a profound challenge to the regime – far greater than their numbers alone might suggest. For despite being a minority within a minority and meeting in secret, they were nevertheless widely talked about, as Shakespeare's dig at them in *Twelfth Night* shows. James instinctively knew that to allow them even the slightest leeway risked undermining the foundations on which Divine Right rested. He asserted that a king was "the author of the law" and that "[k]ings were the makers of the law, not the law of kings". He could not afford to have people saying that God's law was paramount and that their duty was to obey God, not man.

The Court

King James presided over a court notorious for drunken excess. Though no fan of James' successor Charles I, the Puritan Lady Hutchinson contrasted the son's reign favourably with the father's, since "the face of the court was much changed ... for King Charles was temperate and chaste and serious; so that the fools and bawds, mimics and catamites of the former court grew out of fashion, and the nobility and courtiers, who did not quite abandon their debaucheries, had yet that reverence to the king to retire into corners to practise them".

Thee and Thou

By the time work began on the King James Bible, first published in 1611, thee and thou were already falling out of regular English use (though retained to the present day in dialect form). The committee of translators opted to keep them since they match the distinction in Greek and Hebrew between second person familiar and formal, but hotly debated which form to employ when addressing God. They eventually settled on the familiar thee and thou to reflect the fact that He is Father instead of ye and you to reflect that He is also Creator and Lord.

The root of conflict between an authoritarian state on the one hand and Puritans and Separatists on the other was conscience. Divine Right was effectively the will and whim of whoever happened to sit on the throne. If individual conscience was allowed to override what the monarch said, there was no more Divine Right. And since the Bible had such a central role in determining what was permissible for people of conscience, it was vital for officialdom to control it as tightly as possible. The king could not turn back the clock by denying access to the Bible altogether, but he made the best of a bad job with a new translation, the King James or Authorised Version. This killed two birds with one stone,

---

Parliament

King James had an often-fractious relationship with Parliament, telling them that they should "not meddle with the main points of government. That is my craft, and to meddle with it were to lessen me. I am now an old king; for six and thirty years have I governed in Scotland personally, and I have accomplished my apprenticeship here – a great time for a king's experience in government ... I must not be taught my office." For good measure, he warned against raising awkward grievances, for "it is an undutiful part in subjects to press their king, wherein they know beforehand he will refuse them".

Ekklesia

To render the New Testament Greek *ekklesia*, the Geneva Bible used congregation, the King James Bible church. Each term was heavily loaded – one suggesting a self-governing "gathered community" of the kind embraced by Separatists, the other something akin to the traditional bishop-led set-up, emphasising how politically controversial the Bible could be. From the point of view of Divine Right, the word was doubly awkward since *ekklesia* was the citizen assembly of Greek city states, the body in which all free men voted to elect magistrates and set policy.

burnishing his Protestant credentials and playing to his pose as a scholar whilst producing something more congenial to his ideas than the text favoured by Puritans and Separatists.

They used the Geneva Bible, produced in the 1560s by refugees fleeing persecution by Henry VIII's Catholic daughter, Mary Tudor. Based largely on William Tyndale's work, its innovations in style and presentation made it attractive, accessible and affordable – Roman typeface to make it easier to read than traditional Gothic script; chapter and paragraph numbers for the first time in an English-language Bible to make it quicker to find your place and cross-reference; italics to show where words had been inserted to help produce idiomatic English; pocket size to make it suitable for home use; maps, tables and illustrations to produce an all-in-one study guide; and commentaries from some of the best biblical scholars of the day. And there lay the rub. Some of these commentaries verged on incendiary in the eyes of James Stuart. Israel's exodus from Egypt – the delivery of the godly from the hands of a despot. Hebrew

Favourites

James Stuart's treatment of favourites caused great ill feeling over his extravagance and exclusion of Parliament from decision-making. In 1607 the king used £44,000 (a vast sum for the time) to pay off the debts of three friends – resentment of misspending being compounded by the fact that Scots were seen to benefit from money provided by English taxpayers. In 1614 James took up with handsome George Villiers, eventually making him Duke of Buckingham and referring to him as "my only sweet and dear child", "my sweetheart" and "my sweet child and wife".

midwives who ignored Pharaoh's command to murder all Israelite boys – lawful to disobey. The killing of evil Queen Jezebel – an example of how God would deal with tyrants. And plenty more in the same vein. Unsurprisingly, the king made sure commentaries were excluded from the translation of the Scriptures that bore his name, but he could not dim the Geneva Bible's popularity. Under his son Charles I it would eventually sound the death knell for Divine Right.

4

Between a Rock and a Hard Place

"It is not with us as with other men, whom small things can discourage, or small discontents cause to wish themselves home again."

William Bradford

COMPELLED BY THE LOGIC OF his beliefs, King James had not the slightest intention of giving ground to Puritans, let alone the even more extreme Separatists. His suspicion of these groups was rooted in personal antipathy as much as in an opposing religious or philosophical outlook. In them he saw the spiritual kin of Scottish Presbyterians who had been a thorn in his mother's side and had caused him much personal grief. The teacher who had so often beaten him as a boy, George Buchanan, was a Presbyterian charged with moulding the future king into a form acceptable to a Scottish nobility who had forcibly taken him from his mother. And James would have been acutely conscious of the claims made in the previous century by firebrand Scots preacher John Knox, who argued from the Bible that kings did not hold their position as of right, but only by the consent of the people – and, worse, that the people were entitled to depose an unjust or unrighteous king.

Reacting in exasperation to Puritan demands for church reform, James thundered, "I will make them conform themselves, or else I will harry them out of the land, or else do worse." And in

> ### John Knox
> Fearless and combative, Knox admonished Mary, Queen of Scots to her face for supporting Roman Catholic practices, and openly called for her execution after she was implicated in the murder of her husband Lord Darnley. From his pulpit in Edinburgh he thundered, "No manifest idolater ought to be promoted to any public regiment, for neither can oath nor promise bind any such people to obey and maintain tyrants against God. If rashly they have promoted any manifestly wicked person, most justly may the same men depose and punish him."

> ### Enforcing Uniformity
> King James was keen to impose administrative as well as religious conformity across his realms, saying "his wish above all things was at his death to leave one worship to God, one kingdom entirely governed, one uniformity in laws". This was an ambitious undertaking given the diversity between and within his four kingdoms and the resources at the disposal of 17th century monarchs. Though the king asserted, "This I must say for Scotland, and I may truly vaunt it; here I sit and govern it with my pen; I write and it is done," in many respects this was wishful thinking.

this he was as good as his word. Year by year the screw was tightened on those who failed to attend Church of England worship regularly, as legally required. Local authorities which might previously have been prepared to turn a blind eye were now much more zealous in applying the letter of the law, whilst a series of parallel developments signalled an end to any attempt by the king to accommodate Puritan concerns. The icing on the cake was the promulgation of the *Declaration of Sports* in 1618, meeting Puritan desires for stricter Sabbath observance with the exact opposite – a law expressly licensing virtually all the things they wanted banned.

The Declaration of Sports

Puritans believed in strict Sabbath observance and were part of a long-running controversy over sports and games on Sunday afternoons. The 1618 *Declaration of Sports* came down emphatically against them, stating the king's "pleasure likewise is, that after the end of divine service our good people be not disturbed from any lawful recreation, such as dancing, archery, leaping, vaulting – but withal we do here account prohibited all unlawful games: bear- and bull-baiting, interludes [i.e. plays and theatre performances] and bowling".

As the reality of Divine Right played itself out during the reign of James and his son, Puritan views hardened. Theologians began to develop increasingly sophisticated theories of resistance to royal misrule, making common cause with constitutionalists in a foreshadowing of the alliance that would eventually form the backbone of armed rebellion against Charles I. Yet under James this resistance remained passive. St Paul had said, "Everyone must submit himself to the governing authorities, for there is no authority except that which God has established." (Romans 13:1). All the same, to see the institution of government as part of the God-given order for the world was not to say that every act of a particular government had to be approved and endorsed by believers. More and more began to conclude that there were limits on the degree to which Christians should submit to governmental authority, for Jesus' apostles had met state demands by exclaiming, "We must obey God rather than men!" (Acts 5:29). This was certainly the view

---

Opposition to the Crown

Archbishop of Canterbury Richard Bancroft first caused Puritans and constitutionalists to make common cause against the Crown by trying to issue church canons (laws) without Parliamentary approval. Relying on the precedent of the 1559 Act of Uniformity (which gave statutory force to the Thirty-nine Articles, the Church of England's statement of Calvinist orthodoxy) as proof that the right to legislate on church affairs was theirs alone, Members of Parliament objected. Despite first siding with Bancroft, King James eventually backed down.

Dealing with Dissent

Clergymen who did not toe the government line on acceptable doctrine and forms of worship could expect at the very least to be excommunicated like the Scrooby Separatists' preacher Richard Clyfton or stripped of their Church of England posts like their pastor John Robinson, with harsher penalties to follow if they persisted. Meanwhile, a close watch was kept on attendance at Church of England services. Thomas Helwys, who helped with the group's move to Leiden, fell under suspicion simply for failing to take communion at the local church.

Scrooby

An Independent "gathered community" of believers, mostly made up of ordinary country folk, came together in 1606 at Scrooby, in Nottinghamshire. It was led by Pastor John Robinson, noted equally for his learning and tolerant disposition, and Elder William Brewster, who had by then succeeded to his father's position as local postmaster – more prestigious than it sounds since Scrooby lay on the main north-south road and so formed an important communications hub. William Bradford, who later was to become one of the foremost leaders in America, was only a teenager at this point.

---

taken by Separatists, from one congregation of which in north-central England would eventually come the Mayflower Pilgrims.

William Bradford, who in later years was governor of Plymouth colony, wrote of what it meant to be a Separatist trying to live according to their interpretation of biblical teaching during the early part of James Stuart's reign – imprisonment, constant surveillance, being deprived of homes, possessions and livelihoods. Unsurprisingly, his band began to consider following the example of like-minded people who had already sought refuge in Protestant communities abroad. Yet leaving England was easier said than done. Fearful of embittered exiles becoming a focus of opposition and dissent, smuggling in seditious literature and undermining his rule from safe havens overseas, James made it illegal to leave the country without an official permit. Only after several failed attempts during 1607-8, much hardship and the loss of almost all their movable goods did Bradford and his companions eventually quit their homeland.

Exile

William Bradford and those who worshipped with him saw little choice but to leave England: "Yet seeing themselves thus molested, and that there was no hope of their continuance there, by a joint consent they resolved to go into the Low Countries, where they heard was freedom of religion for all men; as also how sundry from London and other parts of the land had been exiled and persecuted for the same cause, and were gone thither, and lived at Amsterdam and in other places of the land. So ... they resolved to get over into Holland as soon as they could."

When at last they did so, they took with them not much more than the clothes on their back and what few belongings they could carry by hand. But for the first time they had the prospect of being able to worship freely, for they were bound for the United Provinces of the Netherlands.

5

A Gilded Cage

"I have been the longer about the description of this place because there are so many particularities wherein it differs (and in some excels)."

Peter Mundy, traveller in Holland, 1640

THE UNITED PROVINCES WERE the wonder of the early 17th century, a land of windmills, dykes and land reclaimed from the sea, almost entirely lacking in natural resources but inhabited by people proverbial for diligence and industry. Still knitting together as a nation, they comprised the northern (Protestant) parts of the former Spanish Netherlands – and despite being engaged in an eighty-year war of liberation against an imperial power that refused to accept their secession, they were in the middle of what proved to be their Golden Age. Reaping the benefits of an economic boom, growing population and vastly expanding trade alongside an extraordinary cultural flowering, the Dutch were carving out a worldwide empire and producing masterpieces of art even as Spanish troops menaced their borders and polders had to be flooded to stop the enemy advance. As well as evolving cutting-edge expertise in ship design and operation, they were innovators in many other areas – in finance, setting up the world's first stock exchange; in science, Lippershey beating Galileo to building the refracting telescope; in

> ### Dutch Life
> The United Provinces was highly urbanised, with 15% living in towns or cities by 1600, compared with 5% across Europe as a whole. The peculiarity of some of its institutions was illustrated by the "drowning cell" attached to Amsterdam's house of correction. In good Calvinist fashion, this aimed to teach the need for hard work to the idle, placing them in a sealed cellar in which there was a tap and a hand pump. Water was let in through the tap, forcing the inmate to pump regularly to keep from drowning.

> ### Shipbuilding
> During the 16th century the Dutch developed a new type of ship for trans-ocean trade: the Fluyt. Built purely for commercial use, it had double the cargo capacity of rival designs, cost half as much to build, required a smaller crew and had a shallower draught. It helped cement Dutch dominance to such an extent that by 1670 the merchant marine of the United Provinces stood at 568,000 tonnes, accounting for about half the European total. Others were steadily frozen out: though the Venetian fleet in 1600 was as big as a century earlier, by the later date half its ships were Dutch-built.

commerce, developing new routes to the Spice Islands and commercialising North Sea fishing; in exploration, discovering Australia and mapping Arctic regions.

Led by their pastor John Robinson, William Bradford and his fellow Separatists set foot in Holland just as a ten-year truce with Spain took effect. They found a nation whose GDP per head was much higher than that of their homeland, providing wealth and a standard of living far beyond what they were used to, with prices to match. Making first for Amsterdam, with its established community of English exiles, they experienced both the heady feeling of freedom and its flipside – for the fractious nature of Dutch political and religious debate was mirrored by infighting amongst the English. They had not escaped persecution at home to be consumed by faction abroad and so, despite the many advantages of Amsterdam – the fastest-growing city in Europe and its foremost centre for shipping, banking and insurance – they soon decamped for nearby Leiden, whose printing and textile trades seemed likely to offer employment.

But restrictive practices closed off those opportunities. Like countless immigrants before and since, they became trapped in low-paying jobs, forced into squalid dwellings, at risk of exploitation. Worse, their children increasingly began to lose their roots, seduced by the materialism of Dutch society, growing more Dutch than English. This was concerning not simply out of sentimentality or cultural prejudice. There was a contradiction at the heart of Dutch society which already hinted at decline – the prosperous burghers depicted in paintings may have worn the sober black of good Calvinists, yet they were also fond of luxuries like

---

Tulips

Between roughly 1600 and 1720 the Dutch had the world's highest per capita income. Amsterdam merchants in particular grew rich on trade to the Spice Islands, where voyages could yield profits of 400%. Among new luxuries which became available on the back of this huge increase in wealth was the tulip. Native to Persia, the flower was prized for the intense colour of its petals. So popular did trading in tulip bulbs become that the Dutch developed what was in effect the first futures contract on the back of it.

The Golden Goose

Loss of the Netherlands was a heavy blow for Spain since taxes from its 200-plus cities (responsible for almost half of all European trade) brought revenue equal to roughly seven times what came from the New World. Eventually a peace concluded by the Union of Arras in 1578 coaxed the southern provinces back under Spanish rule, but the northernmost areas continued in revolt – a division along confessional rather than linguistic lines, for though the southern provinces had a mixture of French and Flemish speakers, they were overwhelmingly Catholic.

Building a Nation

At the outset of the 17th century there was no standard, unified Dutch language. By the end of it, the Dutch had not only created a nation from scratch but set it on secure cultural foundations. Painters such as Rembrandt, Vermeer, Frans Hals, Jacob van Ruisdael and others are household names, but poetry and drama also flourished under men such as Joost van den Vondel (1587-1679), Jacob Cats (1577-1660) and Constantijn Huygens (1596-1687). Pieter Corneliszoon Hooft (1581-1647) recorded these and other achievements in his seminal work of history, *Nederduytsche Historien*.

pipe-smoking, and the portraits in their lavishly furnished homes hinted at vanity. The great theologian John Calvin sounded a warning in one of the Geneva Bible's commentaries: "Let those who have abundance remember that they are surrounded with thorns, and let them take great care not to be pricked by them." It was an apt reminder of the darker side of the Dutch miracle.

As expiry of the truce with imperial Spain drew nearer and the safe haven no longer looked quite so safe, the conviction grew that God was calling His people to move on again. Uprooting themselves a second time was not to be undertaken lightly or for personal advantage. It could be justified only if it was in response to the call of God and preserved the unity and freedom of worship they had won at such cost. After prolonged consideration of the various alternatives, supplemented by much prayer and reading of the Bible, they made their choice – not elsewhere in Europe, but in America. Bradford summed up the excitement which accompanied this decision: "We have great hope and inward zeal of laying some good foundation for the propagating and

advancing of the Gospel of the Kingdom of Christ in these remote parts of the world; yea, though they should be but as stepping-stones to others for performing of so great a work." The challenge was to make intention reality.

6

A Good and Spacious Land

"Heaven and earth never agreed better to frame a place for man's habitation, were it fully manured and inhabited by industrious people."

Captain John Smith

PROSPECTS FOR ENGLISH EXPANsion in the Americas in the 1600s were not promising. South and Central America were firmly within the sphere of influence of Portugal and Spain, who would do all in their power to try and snuff out a colony of interlopers – assuming they managed to survive disease and the harsh climate. In North America the French and Dutch already had settlements and would also be unlikely to look kindly on newcomers in areas they coveted for themselves. Half-hearted English attempts at establishing a viable presence on this continent in the first decades of the century had either

European Settlement in America

Even a century and a half after Columbus' discovery of the New World, there were fewer than half a million Europeans in the whole of the Americas. Of these, around 100,000 were in Brazil, 250,000 in Spanish America and 100,000 (half of them English) in the islands of the Caribbean. At the time the *Mayflower* sailed, North America had a minimal European presence – the French in Canada and the Dutch in Nieuw Nederland numbering probably no more than 1,000 apiece. The English contribution, such as it was, amounted to just a few hundred.

failed outright or been abandoned, except for Jamestown in Virginia – and that was clinging on by its fingernails, becoming the graveyard for thousands of emigrants. During its "starving time" in 1608, 440 out of 500 died in the space of just six months – over 80% mortality.

Stuart colonial policy was effectively to privatise the whole business. In 1606 Virginia (which up till then comprised the eastern seaboard from the

Roanoke

England's early attempts at colonisation in North America were mostly damp squibs or spectacular failures. In 1585 Sir Walter Raleigh sponsored seven ships to carry 89 men and about a third as many women and children to Roanoke Island, in modern North Carolina (then part of Virginia, named for Virgin Queen Elizabeth I). When a relief expedition returned two years later the settlement was abandoned, leaving the word "CROATAN" carved on a tree as the only clue to their fate. To this day, no-one knows for sure what became of the settlers.

Carolinas as far as Massachusetts) was split in two. Monopoly rights in North Virginia (New England) were granted to merchants and fishermen from Plymouth, with the South Virginia equivalent going to London investors (the Virginia Company). The money-men were dazzled by the staggering rates of return which seemed to be on offer – Vasco da Gama's pioneering voyage to India in 1497-9 had earned backers a payback of several hundred per cent, for example. Moreover, Europeans were already developing a taste for New World crops such as potatoes,

> **The Virginia Company**
>
> Thomas Prince's *Chronological History of New England* says the Separatists' negotiations with the Virginia Company were "long delayed" by reason of that body "falling into great disturbances and factions" – a further warning regarding the Company's fitness for the job of spearheading English settlement in North America. The results in Jamestown spoke for themselves: by 1622, only 2,000 of the 10,000 who had sailed to Virginia were still alive. The Company's royal charter was eventually revoked in 1624.

tomatoes, maize and tobacco. An abundance of virgin forest and rich farmland offered opportunities aplenty, whilst the cod fisheries of Newfoundland and the inland fur trade showed the huge potential that existed for exploitation of natural resources.

> **Nieuw Nederland**
>
> Taking advantage of Henry Hudson's 1609 voyage of exploration along the New England coast, the Dutch sent ships each year to the mouth of the River Hudson to trade fur, and by 1614 the Company of Nieuw Nederland had established a colony at Fort Nassau near modern Albany, New Jersey (later moved to Fort Orange). In 1625 New Amsterdam (renamed New York following its 1664 capture by the English) was founded at the southern tip of Manhattan Island and made the seat of government for settlements which by then straddled New York state, New Jersey, Delaware and Connecticut.

Despite the difficulties, politics as well as economics favoured colonisation. It would relieve pressure from a growing population by diverting surplus mouths overseas, creating new sources of supply as the plantations established themselves, and providing an outlet for the ambitions of landless younger sons of the gentry or dissidents of various stripes. It would bind the merchant class to the king, since they stood to gain from opportunities for trade and new markets for English manufactures. It would (or so it was thought) be a way of breaking the Portuguese and Dutch stranglehold on Far East trade and it would help make sure that England was not completely left behind by her European rivals. It was, quite simply, a game King James could not afford to ignore.

By this stage Europeans had explored the Atlantic seaboard of North America as far as the mouth of the St Lawrence River, and in the Pacific knew the outlines of the coast as

> **Looking West**
>
> By uniting the English and Scottish crowns in 1603, King James removed the threat to England of attack from the north. At the same time, after years of difficulty and reverse, English policy in Ireland at last began to make headway. At Kinsale in 1601 the forces of the native Irish confederates under Hugh O'Neill and Red Hugh O'Donnell, together with a Spanish army that had come to their aid, was decisively defeated. The subsequent peace treaty with Spain and surrender of remaining Irish forces opened the way for a new English effort to colonise North America.

far north as modern Washington State. Because of their yearly trips to the cod fisheries of the north-east, Englishmen had had intermittent contact with Native

---

Prospero and Caliban

For *The Tempest*, Shakespeare drew on the shipwreck of the Virginia Company's flagship *The Sea Venture* off Bermuda in 1609 during an ill-fated attempt to resupply Jamestown. The play – probably written in 1611 but not published until 1623 – offers a contemporary perspective on the inhabitants of the New World, with the misshapen Caliban, offspring of a witch, kept bound by Prospero and made sport of by Europeans shipwrecked on the magician's island. It is entirely possible Shakespeare had seen Native Americans who – like Squanto [q.v.] – had been brought to Europe.

American tribes in those parts (though knowledge of them remained scant) and several accounts of the New World had been published. The interior was for the greater part unknown, but a growing body of information was available nevertheless, with Captain John Smith – leveraging the fame of his Jamestown escapades and experience won during his voyages of exploration – acting as one of the main cheerleaders for English settlement.

Yet despite the use of indentured servitude (with investors paying the passage of people who could not afford it in return for their working unpaid in America for an agreed period), manpower and skills shortages were endemic. From Jamestown, Smith himself had written despairingly back to London that he would rather the Virginia Company sent out "thirty carpenters, husbandmen, gardeners, blacksmiths, masons and diggers-up of tree roots, well provided, than a thousand such as we have". That plantation's dismal performance confirmed that something needed to change.

Smallpox

European diseases devastated Native American populations with no resistance to them. Adriaen van der Donck, a Dutchman living in the Hudson valley heartland of Nieuw Nederland in the 1640s, wrote of the effects on the surrounding tribes, who "affirm that, before the arrival of the Christians, and before the smallpox broke out among them, they were ten times as numerous as they are now; and that their population had been melted down by this disease, whereof nine-tenths of them have died". It seems to have been a similar story across swathes of the continent.

The 1618 comet

Wikimedia Commons

Illustration from James Stuart's book *Daemonology*,
showing witches being brought before the king

Wikimedia Commons

THE BIBLE

AND

HOLY SCRIPTVRES

CONTEYNED IN

THE OLDE AND NEWE

Teſtament.

TRANSLATED ACCOR-

ding to the Ebrue and Greke, and conferred With

the beſt tranſlations in diuers langages.

WITH MOSTE PROFITABLE ANNOTA-

tions vpon all the hard places, and other things of great

importance as may appeare in the Epiſtle to the Reader.

FEARE IL NOT, STAND STIL, AND BEHOLDE

the ſaluacion of the Lord, which he wil forw. to you this day. Exod. 14.13.

THE LORD SHAL FIGHT FOR YOV: THEREFORE

holde you your peace. Exod. 14. ver. 14.

AT GENEVA.

PRINTED BY ROVLAND HALL

M·D·LX·

Geneva Bible

Wikimedia Commons

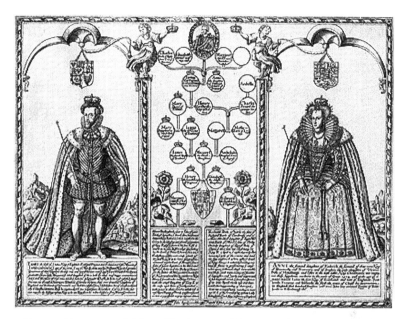

James Stuart and his wife Anne of Denmark. Engraving by
Renold Elstrack (1570-1625), National Gallery of Art,
Washington DC.

Wikimedia Commons

De Champlain's 1612 engraving of Algonquin tribespeople in
southern New England

Wikimedia Commons

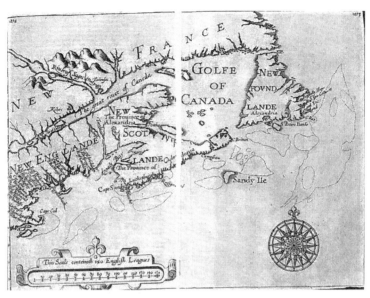

A map of the New England and Newfoundland coastline
appearing in the 1625 edition of *Purchas his Pilgrimes,
Contayning a history of the world, in sea voyages*
Wikimedia Commons

The Mayflower

In ye name of God Amen. We whose names are underwritten, the loyall subjects of our dread soueraigne Lord King Iames by ye grace of god, of great Britaine, franc, & Ireland king, defendor of ye faith, &c

Haueing undertaken, for ye glorie of god, and advancemente of ye Christian faith, and honour of our king & countrie, a voyage to plant ye first colonie in ye Northerne parts of Virginia. Doe by these presents solemnly & mutualy in ye presence of god, and one of another, couenant, & combine our selues togeather into a ciuill body politick, for our better ordering, & preseruation & furtherance of ye ends aforesaid; and by vertue hearof to enacte, constitute, and frame shuch just & equall lawes, ordinances, Acts, constitutions, & offices, from time to time, as shall be thought most meete & conuenient for ye generall good of ye Colonie: unto which we promise all due submission and obedience. In witnes wherof we haue hereunder subscribed our names at Cap= Codd ye .11. of Nouember, in ye year of ye raigne of our soueraigne Lord King Iames of England, franc, & Ireland ye eighteenth and of Scotland ye fiftie fourth. An: Dom. 1620.

The Mayflower Compact

Wikimedia Commons

31

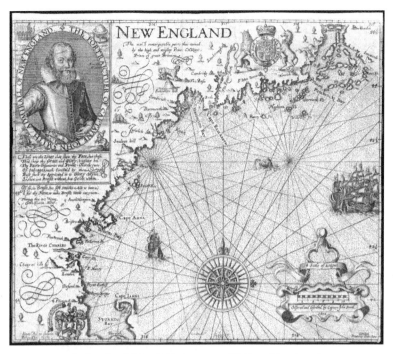

John Smith's 1614 map of New England

Wikimedia Commons

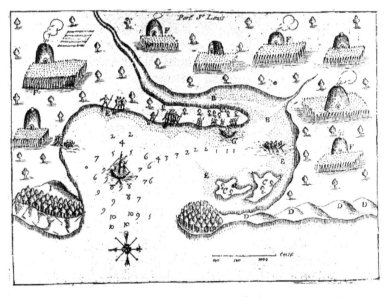

Samuel de Champlain's 1605 map of Plymouth Harbour,
Pilgrim Museum

Wikimedia Commons

7

Pilgrims and Strangers

"Let your wisdom and godliness appear not only in choosing such persons as do entirely love and will promote the common good, but also in yielding unto them all due honour and obedience in their lawful administration."

Pastor John Robinson

AGAINST THIS BACKGROUND the Leiden Separatists considered their options. They needed backing from King James, as settlement within areas owing him allegiance would bring royal protection – vital not so much against the local inhabitants as against jealous European rivals. It would also open the way to funding from English investors. On the other hand, this ran the risk that they would once again be persecuted for their religious beliefs. To square the circle, they decided that they would (as Bradford put it) "live in a distinct body by ourselves, under the general government of Virginia, and … [ask] His Majesty to grant us free liberty and freedom of religion". Depending on one's viewpoint, this was a plan of astounding naivety, pig-headedness or boldness, for they were effectively asking the king to grant overseas what he had consistently refused at home. Nothing in James Stuart's behaviour to date suggested any reason to believe he would agree to it.

Feelers put out to test their chance of being allowed to settle in Virginia

> ### The Spanish Threat
> Renewal of war with Spain was a frightening prospect. The conflict had been long and bloody, and all were at risk either of conscription or of suffering atrocities – the armies of His Most Catholic Majesty seldom having shown much sympathy towards people who were not only rebels, but also heretics. It was far from inevitable that the Dutch would withstand a renewed Spanish onslaught. If Spain won, the Roman Catholic church would become the state church of the United Provinces, the Inquisition would have free rein and what the Separatists had suffered in England would pale in comparison.

> ### Rivals and Realpolitik
> The idea of Dutchmen using English Separatists to aid the expansion of Nieuw Nederland seems to have foundered on a hard-headed assessment of how this would damage relations with King James. Under Elizabeth I England had been one of Holland's few allies against the Spanish, and the Dutch regime had no wish to antagonise her successor. The United Provinces were already treading a fine line by sheltering religious dissidents, the more so since material the English government considered seditious was often printed by these emigrants and smuggled to sympathisers at home.

quickly ran into trouble, the task of changing the king's mind being unexpectedly made more difficult when royal agents traced critical pamphlets that had been smuggled into England back to William Brewster, one of the Leiden exiles. Negotiations stalled, but they had allies in unexpected places. The Privy Council, the king's closest and most trusted advisers, included men of Puritan (if not exactly Separatist) sympathies – financier Sir John Wolstenholme, Chancellor of the Exchequer Fulke Greville and Secretary of State Sir Robert Naunton. Whilst Naunton dragged his feet over the smuggled pamphlets, the trio worked to convince James that it would be to his advantage to let the Pilgrims go.

There were persuasive arguments on that score: the Virginia plantation desperately needed settlers, especially families and single women; introducing a community of proven cohesiveness, toughness and industriousness was a chance to extend areas under the king's control; if James did not support people who were still nominally his subjects, the Dutch might do so, using them to found a colony in competition with the English; it would keep the Separatists out of harm's way, for whilst they could smuggle pamphlets easily from Leiden to England, that was impractical from America; and it would be self-financing, requiring James to put up no cash. On being told that the Pilgrims intended to earn their living by fishing, the monarch reportedly exclaimed, "So God have my soul, 'tis an honest trade – the Apostles' own calling." But on freedom of religion, he would give no firm commitment, saying only, "I will connive at them and not molest them, provided they conduct themselves

---

Freedom of Speech

William Brewster got into trouble after publishing material critical of King James' attempts to impose bishops on Scotland. His home was raided, a fellow-printer arrested, equipment seized and Brewster forced into hiding. This came at a critical time during 1619, as the Separatists' arrangements for emigration to America were being finalised. A senior and well-respected member of the community, Brewster would ordinarily have played a significant part in the ongoing negotiations with potential financiers, but others had to take his place, primarily John Carver and Robert Cushman.

The Privy Council

There were 40 members of Elizabeth I's Privy Council in 1553 but membership was almost halved under King James, as this body lost ground to royal favourites like the Duke of Buckingham. Fuelling English concern was the fact that though James included stalwarts of their aristocracy like the earls of Suffolk, Dorset, Somerset and Essex, he added what some regarded as a disproportionate number of Scottish nobles. Office-holders like Chancellor of the Exchequer, Attorney-General and Secretary of State – present *ex officio* – were seen as a poor counterbalance.

Sir John Wolstenholme

One of the richest merchants in London, Sir John Wolstenholme played a significant role in English overseas expansion, helping incorporate the East India Company, sponsoring lectures on navigation and funding a succession of attempts to find a north-west passage. Knighted in 1617, he briefly fell from favour but by 1624 was a commissioner for winding up the Virginia Company. His interest in American affairs continued as a member of King James' council for Virginia and in 1631 he was made commissioner for the plantation of Virginia.

Strangers

People brought in by the Virginia Company, all of whom had originally been destined for Jamestown, included hired hands, servants, farmers, tanners, weavers, shopkeepers and even four children. The Company started transporting children (usually orphans, foundlings, the illegitimate or those whose families were receiving poor relief) as indentured servants in 1618. Three of the four children on the *Mayflower* died during their first winter in the New World, but a fourth (Richard More) lived to the age of 81.

---

peaceably; but to allow or tolerate them under my seal, that I will not consent to do." With that they had no choice but to be content.

Through the latter part of 1618 and throughout the following year preparations for leaving began in earnest. The Leiden Separatists were poor and their funds limited, and though they numbered many hundreds, not all were fit and able to undertake a passage to America straight away. As a result, they had no option but to seek money from outside investors, with two main consequences. Firstly, they were compelled to agree that they would spend the initial seven years in America working to pay off their backers. Secondly, they were obliged to water down what had always been intended as a godly venture. In the event, roughly half the *Mayflower's* passengers were economic migrants, brought in by the Merchant Adventurers to make up the numbers and form an economically viable settlement. These outsiders – called "strangers" by the Pilgrims – were to prove a constant source of discord.

Yet despite all obstacles, by mid-1620 they were on their way from Leiden to England, there to take ship

---

Leaving Holland

In his *History of Plymouth Plantation* William Bradford describes the Pilgrims' leaving Holland to take ship for England and onward to America: "[A] sad and mournful parting; to see what sighs and sobs and prayers did sound among them; what tears did gush from every eye, and pithy speeches pierced each other's hearts; that sundry of the Dutch strangers, that stood on the quay as spectators, could not refrain from tears. Yet comfortable and sweet it was to see such lively and true expressions of dear and unfeigned love."

---

for the New World. William Bradford described the departure with customary emphasis on their spiritual objective: "So they left the goodly and pleasant city, which had been their resting-place these many years; they knew they were pilgrims, and looked not much on those outward things, but lifted up their eyes to the heavens, their dearest country, and quieted their spirits."

8

A Storm-Tossed Sea

"I'll warrant him for drowning, though the ship were no stronger than a nutshell, and as leaky as an unstanched wench."

Shakespeare, The Tempest

THE 2,750-MILE VOYAGE ACROSS the Atlantic to America was a risky undertaking at the best of times and under the most favourable conditions, almost standing comparison with modern space travel. Battling contrary winds and currents, the *Mayflower* took 66 days to reach Cape Cod – not especially long by the standards of the day, but particularly gruelling considering that most of her passengers had been on board almost continually for the best part of two months before she eventually set sail on 6 September 1620. Allowing for shore breaks when the ship docked at Southampton, Plymouth and Dartmouth, many may have spent almost 120 days at sea. By comparison, in 1969 the Mariner 7 probe took only 131 days to make the journey to Mars. Cramped conditions below decks, lack of air and privacy, poor diet and the rigours of mountainous seas and violent storms were not eased by tensions between crew, strangers and Pilgrims.

> **Peril on the High Seas**
>
> At sea the Pilgrims were not only at risk from the actions of the wind and waves. Throughout the first half of the 1600s, pirates from the Barbary Coast in North Africa (modern Libya, Tunisia, Algeria and Morocco) plagued the coasts around Britain and Ireland. Admiralty records show 466 vessels seized between 1609 and 1616, with another 27 taken near Plymouth in 1625. On occasion, pirates would even come ashore seeking plunder and captives – the latter being enslaved and often forcibly converted to Islam.

> **False Starts**
>
> When the *Mayflower* sailed from England's south coast port of Plymouth on 6 September 1620 it was a case of third time lucky. The expedition first got under way on 5 August, only to find within a few days that the Speedwell was taking in water. They put back to Dartmouth for repairs, but on setting out again were not much more than 300 miles into the Atlantic before once again this ill-starred vessel proved (as William Bradford put it) "so leaky as [we] must bear up or sink at sea". Back again they went, this time giving up the Speedwell as a lost cause.

Dogged by mishaps and bad luck, the would-be settlers were almost comically ill-prepared for what lay ahead. Departure was several times delayed when a backup ship (the Speedwell) proved to leak like a sieve. Valuable rations were consumed whilst trying to make repairs, with stores needed for America being sold to pay bills and meet other expenses – all in vain, for the vessel eventually had to be abandoned, forcing everyone to crowd onto the *Mayflower* and robbing them of the means of fishing when they made landfall. The late sailing meant there would be no time to plant and harvest before winter came on, though in any event they had not the slightest knowledge of New World farming

---

The Ships

Built in 1577, the Speedwell was a death-trap. Over 40 years old in an age when the normal working life of ships plying European waters was about 15 years, she was unseaworthy and a danger to all who set sail in her. The *Mayflower*, built in 1609, was in every respect far superior, but even she had a design fundamentally unsuitable for the task in hand. High castle-like structures fore and aft made it difficult to sail against the prevailing westerly winds of the North Atlantic, adding to the length and discomfort of the crossing.

---

techniques and crops. The most basic planning and provision were defective in other ways, too, for whilst they took pigs, goats and poultry, there were no draught animals or horses, no butter or oil, no contingency reserves. Even armour and weapons were in short supply. Dispassionate observers would have been forgiven for thinking the enterprise doomed before it started.

Life Aboard

The *Mayflower's* passengers lived mostly on the gun deck, whose length stem to stern was about 80 feet. Since 12 feet or so of this was used for storing powder and shot, that left 1,600 square feet or thereabouts available between 102 of them – just over 13 square feet per person or barely three and a half feet by four, with about five feet of headroom. Presumably hammocks would have been used at night to allow sufficient space for all to sleep – hammocks having been formally adopted by the Royal Navy in 1597.

Yet despite running into a gale so severe that passengers were pressed into service to help repair a broken mast, mortality during the voyage was astoundingly low. This was an era when up to half of those aboard might expect to die on such a voyage, but only two were lost – a young servant and a sailor described by Bradford as "a proud and very profane young man" who had

felt "the just hand of God upon him". If this verged on miraculous, more so was the experience of John Howland, who fell into raging seas yet managed to keep hold of a length of rope and, incredibly, was brought back on board alive. Despite lying ill for some days, he survived, later marrying fellow Separatist Elizabeth Tilley. From their ten children and more than eighty grandchildren are descended Presidents Franklin Delano Roosevelt, George

Master Mariner Jones

Born in 1570, Captain Christopher Jones died within a year of arriving home in London after taking the Pilgrims to America, his health broken by the privations suffered on that voyage and his mind no doubt haunted by the memory of dead shipmates – a third of the *Mayflower's* crew never made it back. As part owner of the ship he was a man of some means and his widow and young children are unlikely to have been left destitute, though little is known of what became of them after his death. Jones is buried in St Mary's church, Rotherhithe, east London.

H.W. Bush and George W. Bush, poets Ralph Waldo Emerson and Henry Wadsworth Longfellow, actors Alec Baldwin, Humphrey Bogart and Christopher

Navigation

Ships could make eight knots when wind and sea were set fair, considerably less at other times, with knowledge of how best to use the Gulf Stream and other winds and currents still in its infancy. Ready reckoning was still the order of the day: latitude could be gauged reasonably accurately, but working out longitude was largely guesswork. The *Mayflower* was more than three hundred miles off course when she eventually made landfall on the North American coast – five hundred miles away from the nearest English settlements at Jamestown in the south and Newfoundland in the north.

Lloyd, founder of Mormonism Joseph Smith and child care guru Dr Benjamin Spock. Today some two million Americans can count them as ancestors.

All the same, the voyage took a heavy toll on both passengers and crew. By the time they sighted land on 9 November 1620 many were in a weakened condition. Moreover, they had been blown way off course. Instead of being in Virginia plantation, they were hundreds of miles north – an error they were prevented from correcting by dangerous shoals and breakers as they sought to tack south. This was no mere technicality. Being outside their licensed zone of settlement imperilled everything, calling into question the legality of what they were doing – hence what protection they could expect from the Crown and the future security and the viability of their colony. Yet bad though that was, it paled alongside even more immediate and pressing concerns. Whilst on one side the captain and crew of the *Mayflower* threatened to abandon them and their belongings on shore and sail back to England, on the other some of the strangers threatened mutiny.

Danger Ashore

The threat to settlements without royal protection was very real. A Huguenot (French Protestant) colony in what is now South Carolina was destroyed in the 1560s by Dominique de Gourges (who went on to found the first Spanish colony in Florida), the entire population being hanged as heretics. This happened at a time when France and Spain had brought a long-running war to an end, but it seems either that Gourges had not heard about the peace or felt free to act anyway, knowing that the French regime did not look kindly on Huguenots.

9

The Mayflower Compact

"We do by these presents ... covenant and combine ourselves together into a civil body politic ... for the general good of the Colony, unto which we promise all due submission and obedience."

The Mayflower Compact

A COMPLETE BREAKDOWN OF order and discipline was the last thing they needed. Strangers had been a source of friction throughout the voyage. Now, released from undertakings to the Virginia Company, they endangered the whole enterprise by claiming the right to do exactly as they pleased once ashore. Separatist leaders knew they had to get a grip on this, and quickly. Elder William Brewster – once assistant to Elizabeth I's Secretary of State – no doubt was instrumental in helping hammer out a solution. The answer: an agreement we know as the *Mayflower Compact*. In slightly under two hundred words, signed in the captain's cabin by all heads of household and adult males on board, it described the founding principles of the new colony. No-one knows for sure who wrote it, though Brewster's background and skills make him the most likely candidate.

> **William Brewster**
>
> Graduating from Cambridge University's Peterhouse College, Brewster became assistant to diplomat William Davison. The luckless Davison was later imprisoned – ostensibly for exceeding his remit as a member of the commission Elizabeth I set up to try Mary Queen of Scots for plotting against her, more probably being made a scapegoat after Mary was executed. Brewster seems to have come out of this affair unscathed, though under James Stuart he got into trouble for publishing material the king disapproved of.

> **Calendars**
>
> The *Mayflower Compact* was signed within three days of land first being sighted and is dated 11 November 1620 (our 21 November) because at that time England was still using the Julian calendar, which by that stage was ten days behind the Gregorian calendar of today. England did not move to the more accurate Gregorian calendar until well over a century later under the Calendar (New Style) Act of 1750 – a change accompanied by riots as people protested at having days (as they thought) stolen from them.

Before leaving Leiden, pastor John Robinson had advised the Pilgrims that they should reorganise to "become a body politic, using amongst yourselves civil government". The Compact effected that transition, drawing on examples positive and negative; applying principles from their experiences as a religious community; adapting tried and trusted forms to suit a situation for which there was no precedent. This is what Bradford later described as "such government and governors as we should by common consent agree to make and choose" – a voluntary, binding coming together under laws which would in due course be drawn up by their elected officials.

> **Compulsion or Consent?**
> The signatories of the *Mayflower Compact* were subjects of a king who thought he had the right to compel obedience. It was utterly revolutionary for them to put in place a system of government in which they chose their own leaders and decided for themselves how to order their affairs. Unlike James Stuart, who saw himself as answerable to no man, those in positions of authority were to be accountable to the people who had chosen them. Consent, not compulsion, lay at the heart of what the new colony was to be.

The Compact is the future United States in embryo: rooted in the consent of the governed, grounded in the idea that obedience to the law requires freely given assent. And for believers in Divine Right, it is the nightmare of Puritanism made flesh. To all practical purposes the new colony was beyond the reach of King James geographically. By ensuring that ideas and practices which Separatists applied to church affairs would also be used to direct secular life, the *Mayflower Compact* put it beyond his reach in a way that was ultimately much more profound: ideologically – a direction of travel straight away confirmed by election of one of the Separatists, John Carver, as governor, succeeded on his death a short while

> **Democracy**
> Influential Protestant theologian Jean Calvin saw a democratic framework in the history of ancient Israel. Commenting on the leadership structure and judicial arrangements put in place after the Israelites fled captivity in Egypt (Deuteronomy 1:14-16), he observed, "...it appears that those who were to preside in judgment were not appointed only by the will of Moses, but elected by the votes of the people." Puritans noted also that Israel's leaders were subject to the same law as everyone else, concluding that a ruler's authority was under judgment and his power was limited.

later by William Bradford.

Despite formulaic declarations of loyalty to the Crown, the Compact's provisions are at odds with the kind of monarchy James Stuart embodied, built as they are around concepts that were explosive in Puritan hands: covenant and consent. Each Separatist had made a personal covenant (agreement or contract) with God by swearing loyalty and allegiance to Him but they were

> **Trusting the King**
> In *The True Law of Free Monarchies*, King James claimed that, although it was prudent for a monarch "to follow his own laws, as a show of good faith to his subjects, this is not required of him, for a king is only accountable to God". The implication was that James believed a monarch could do precisely as he pleased without regard to any undertakings he might previously have given. That boded ill for the *Mayflower* Separatists, suggesting the king would force religious conformity on them when he thought the time was right.

also covenanted to each other, meaning that all took part in and were responsible for the common religious life of their community. King James' publication *The True Law of Free Monarchies* – his manifesto for Divine Right of kings – had uniformity at the expense of diversity, position based on birth rather than merit, top-down control instead of allowing ordinary people a voice. But Separatists took completely the opposite view. The Bible told them that all human beings were created equal, subject to the same divine laws and dependent alike on Christ for their redemption, the logical conclusion being that all deserved an equal say, nobody should be above the law and no-one should lord it over others.

Just as a spiritual covenant underpinned the Leiden congregation, so their new colony was founded on a secular covenant, bringing with it the germ of democracy, for the rationale of biblical teaching was totally at odds with despotism. If "prophesying" was allowed in church meetings, why not have a similar right in politics? If the only biblically sanctioned organisational unit was the congregation, why should their colony defer to any higher authority? If accepting Christ required choice and consent, why not the same for a government? King James was right all along – no bishops, no king.

Toleration

Puritanism ran the gamut from the prescriptiveness of Presbyterianism to the tolerance (unusual for its time) of Separatists and Independents. In 1612 Thomas Helwys could write that as the power of a monarch "extends to all the goods and bodies of his servants but not to their spirits ... Let them be heretics, Turks, Jews, or whatsoever, it appertains not to the earthly power to punish them in the least measure." In 1614 Thomas Butcher agreed: "...the king and Parliament may please to permit all sorts of Christians, yea, Jews, Turks and pagans, so long as they are peaceable and no malefactors."

The Protestant Ethic

Puritan ideas on work and learning permeated New England society. Literacy (to enable reading of the Bible) and wider education (to provide context for understanding what it said) were both prized, alongside practical and scientific knowledge. God's command to "work [the earth] and take care of it" (Genesis 2:15) was taken to mean a duty to explore Creation; a requirement to "work out [their] salvation with fear and trembling" (Philippians 2:12) implied hard work and personal responsibility; diligence in performing even the most mundane tasks was treated as an act of worship.

10

Against the Odds

"If they had been mindful of that country, from whence they came out, they had leisure to have returned. But now they desire a better, that is an heavenly country."

Book of Hebrews, New Testament

THE PILGRIMS HAD BEEN FORTUnate indeed to have made landfall far from their intended destination. Divine Right was not simply an uncomfortable bedfellow for *Magna Carta*, rule of law and freedom of conscience, but their polar opposite. Their ability to worship as they pleased was unlikely long to survive contact with it, and King James had studiously avoided giving any firm commitment on that score. It was the happy accident of making landfall outside their sanctioned area of settlement which left the Pilgrims in legal limbo and allowed them to pursue their own model of government without outside interference. In the first months and years in New England, however, issues of that kind took second place to mere survival.

Assailed by the harsh winter, weakened by all they had suffered during the sea voyage, and exposed to the elements as they explored the country and started to build dwellings and defences, one by one they sickened and died. By spring they had buried over half their number. That the remainder did not quickly follow them was due to one outlandish piece of good fortune after another, not least the discovery of winter grain stores buried by local

> **Battling the Elements**
>
> As New Plymouth struggled to establish itself during the winter of 1620-21, the settlers were under pressure from severe cold as well as starvation and disease. Much of the globe experienced extreme conditions at that time – for several months, lakes and rivers in Europe froze hard enough to bear the weight of loaded carts, and people were able to walk between Europe and Asia over the ice that covered the Bosphorus. Drought caused crop failure in the Chesapeake basin, bringing Jamestown almost to its knees. It was a miracle New Plymouth did not follow suit.

> **First Encounter Beach**
>
> A landing party from the *Mayflower* was attacked on what is now called First Encounter beach, conceivably because the English had dug up some mounds they saw near an abandoned village, taking away stored food and disturbing graves. Edward Winslow, however, ascribes the hostility to an English ship's captain called Hunt, who had visited the area some while earlier, pretending to trade before capturing a number of natives and selling them as slaves for £20 apiece. It was this same Captain Hunt who had first abducted Squanto [q.v.].

tribespeople, without which they would have starved. What none of them knew when they first set foot on American soil was that only two years earlier a majority of the coastal New England tribes had been almost wiped out by disease, hence the abandoned villages their reconnaissance parties found and the locals' failure to renew the attack which had met one of their initial probes along the coastline.

Perhaps most extraordinary of all, into their midst on 16 March 1621 strode Samoset, a tribal chief who spoke English learnt from fishermen who came each year to catch migrating cod. His visit was an amazing chance, for he ordinarily lived in Maine but was in the area to see the sachem Massasoit (a.k.a. Ousamequin), chief of the Wampanoag whose lands these were. He explained that nearby lived Tisquantum (Squanto, as the English called him), who spoke better English and whom Samoset would bring to visit them. He was as good as his word, returning a few days later with Squanto. To a people accustomed to seeing the workings of God in all things, this must have seemed an answer to prayer. Captured by the English as a young man and taken to England, where he was trained as a guide and interpreter and later joined Captain John Smith on an expedition to New England, Squanto had only recently come back to the land of his birth. Tragically, he arrived to find his own tribe, the Patuxets, had been obliterated by disease.

Squanto was vital to the success of Plymouth Plantation. By teaching the settlers how to cultivate maize using a local fish to fertilise the soil, he ensured that they could feed themselves. Guiding the Pilgrims in an unfamiliar landscape, and describing its flora and fauna, he helped them survive in a

---

Native Americans

Disease was not the only thing to devastate the Native Americans of New England. In a 1621 sermon preached at New Plymouth, Robert Cushman observed that the local tribes "were very much wasted of late, by reason of a great mortality that fell amongst them three years since, which together with their own civil dissentions and bloody wars hath so wasted them, as I think the twentieth person is scarce left alive". Population figures are at best speculative, but in 1600 there may have been as few as one million Native Americans in the whole of North America.

Squanto

The motives of Squanto are opaque. In *Good News from New England* Edward Winslow says the settlers "by degrees ... began to discover Tisquantum", whose aim was "only to make himself great in the eyes of his countrymen, by means of his nearness and favour with us, not caring who fell so [long as] he stood. In the general, his course was to persuade them he could lead us to peace or to war at his pleasure, and would oft threaten the Indians, sending them word in a private manner, we were intended shortly to kill them, that thereby he might get gifts to himself to work to their peace."

Massasoit

Leader of the Wampanoag Confederacy was Massasoit, meaning "great chief". The treaty he agreed with the English included a provision that neither side should "injure or do hurt" to the other. Peace lasted as long as Massasoit ruled, the colonists' relationship with him being greatly helped when the chief fell ill in 1623 and was nursed back to health by Edward Winslow. On his recovery, Massasoit exclaimed that "the English are my friends and love me" and that "whilst I live, I will never forget this kindness they have showed me".

potentially hostile environment. Acting as their intermediary and translator, he was instrumental in the making of a treaty with Massasoit which lifted the daily threat of attack and gave the newcomers legitimacy in their neighbours' eyes. And, even here, circumstances were on the side of the English, for pressures on the Wampanoag by competing tribes made an alliance attractive to them. After months of uncertainty, at last the new arrivals had a firm foundation on which to build.

The *Mayflower's* passengers found no gold, silver or gems; their plans to make a living from fishing came to naught; many of them had died and those who remained would for many years eke out a precarious living. But they had overcome many obstacles and they were free. As they celebrated the first Thanksgiving on 21 November 1621 – a day marked by prayer, fasting and repentance – they could have been forgiven for thinking that the hand of the Lord had been on them.

11

Building Jerusalem

"American democracy is not founded on the emancipated man but, quite the contrary, on the kingdom of God and the limitation of all earthly powers by the sovereignty of God."

Dietrich Bonhöffer

THE TREATY WITH MASSASOIT was the last service John Carver was able to perform for his companions, as the Governor shortly afterwards succumbed to sickness (apparently brought on by sunstroke). So, the responsibility of steering the infant colony through its early years and making a practical reality of the principles enshrined in the *Mayflower Compact* fell to his successor William Bradford. He and his fellow Pilgrims were clear on one thing from the start: there was to be separation of church and state, with marriage a civil ceremony, as it was in the Netherlands. They still had painful memories of how King James used ecclesiastical courts to impose his own views on permissible forms of worship to their detriment, and wanted no repeat – a model later adopted by the United States.

> **Governor Bradford**
>
> The proper line of demarcation between church and state was clear in William Bradford's mind: if things were "nowhere found in the Gospel to be laid on the ministers as a part of their office", then these fell within the remit of the civil power – an approach quite different from that later adopted by the Massachusetts Bay colony, where pastors had a say in the commonwealth's day-to-day affairs. By contrast, though biblical principles were to guide all aspects of the running of New Plymouth, this was not to be a theocracy.

> **Pilgrim Fathers**
>
> The name Pilgrim Fathers only came into vogue some two centuries after the *Mayflower* sailed, her Separatist passengers never using the phrase. Instead they called themselves Saints, meaning people of God. Writing his history of Plymouth Plantation in the 1630s, William Bradford referred to pilgrims because of the connotation of being a wanderer in pursuit of a holy objective – phraseology taken up by Cotton Mather and others of later generations so that it became common in New England to talk of the sons or heirs of the Pilgrims.

Years later the plantation's legal status was formalised by issue of the Warwick Patent under Charles I, but the *Mayflower Compact* continued to be revered as a cornerstone of their constitution. John Quincy Adams – who was himself educated in Leiden whilst his father served as ambassador to the Netherlands – observed, "This is perhaps the only instance in human history of that positive, original social compact, which

45

speculative philosophers have imagined as the only legitimate source of government. Here was a unanimous and personal assent by all the individuals of the community, to the association by which they became a nation." In large measure its principles set the tone for New England as a whole and even for the wider nation, harking back as they did to *Magna Carta* and the traditional freedoms of Englishmen and women. They helped

> **Magna Carta**
>
> Charters drawn up by many early American colonies were modelled on *Magna Carta*, the bedrock of English freedoms, to which Puritans and constitutionalists in England increasingly referred in their efforts to restrain Stuart despotism. The seal of the Massachusetts Bay colony included a militiaman with sword in one hand and *Magna Carta* in the other, prefiguring American Revolutionaries' slogan of "no taxation without representation" – a phrase first appearing in an amendment to *Magna Carta* issued by King Edward I (reigned 1272-1307).

ensure that when England herself was embroiled in civil war in 1642, large numbers from New England returned to the mother country to fight for Parliament against royal tyranny, amongst them many of the first graduates from Harvard.

> **The Great Migration**
>
> When John Winthrop began organising the 1630 Great Migration of Puritans to New England, he carefully avoided earlier settlers' mistakes. The Massachusetts Bay Company was a hard-headed commercial undertaking, founded in London in 1628 as a joint stock company. Backed by wealthy merchants of Puritan persuasion, it aimed not just to implement a divine scheme in the New World, but to turn a profit in the process – a typically Puritan combination of the other-worldly and the decidedly secular.

By the end of his life Bradford could have been excused for looking back with pride on all that he and his fellow Separatists had achieved. Although by then Plymouth Plantation had long been eclipsed by the Massachusetts Bay Colony – John Winthrop's Puritan foundation to the north – the First Comers had nevertheless put themselves on a secure footing, growing well beyond the original settlement's boundaries and achieving greater wealth than they could have hoped for had they stayed at home. Moreover, they and their fellow New Englanders were already starting to outdo the English colonies further south – despite receiving fewer immigrants, New England's population exceeded that of Virginia and Maryland by the dawn of the eighteenth century.

> **Population Growth**
>
> During the entire 17th century New England received only 21,000 emigrants, whilst 120,000 went to Virginia and Maryland. Yet by 1700 New England's population of 91,000 (a six-fold increase in two generations) was greater, Virginia and Maryland between them having 6,000 fewer people. This was because people lived longer in the north, where those who survived infancy could expect to reach the age of 70, whilst few made it beyond 40 in the south – reflecting not just a healthier climate but also better education and a more even distribution of wealth.

It was typical of the Separatist mind, however, that Bradford was unimpressed by material success. Towards the end of his long life he was, if anything, deeply disappointed that his hopes appeared not to have been achieved. Instead of winning Native Americans to Christ by example and preaching of the Gospel, too often the tribes had been treated shamefully, as Christian teaching time and again gave way to expediency and the ways of the world – and this by people from New Plymouth, not just by outsiders. Rather than removing their youngsters from temptation by leaving the ungodly United Provinces, the Separatists saw them fall more and more into the trap of greed and materialism. And though they had sought to distance themselves from a repressive regime and gain freedom to serve God and worship as they pleased, intolerance could be an ugly sore in their own communities, too.

The congregation from Leiden had made the journey across the sea with pure motives, seeking first and foremost to do the will of God. They achieved much, but in other ways fell short, as humans inevitably do. They did not perhaps build a New Jerusalem, yet what was done by them and through them deserves remembrance all the same. As Bradford put it, "May not and ought not the children of these fathers rightly say: Our fathers were Englishmen which came across this great ocean, and were ready to perish in this wilderness, but they cried unto the Lord, and he heard their voice, and looked on their adversity."

12

Thanksgiving

"Though I bequeath you no estate, I leave you in the enjoyment of liberty."

William Bradford

A FOUR-DAY HOLIDAY, GREAT food, time with family, chance to reflect on the past... Though Thanksgiving today is as much a secular event as a religious festival, its North American roots are firmly anchored in the Mayflower Pilgrims' early experiences in the New World. As with so much else they devised in response to novel threats and new challenges, they took something familiar – King James had called a Day of Thanksgiving in 1606 after failure of the previous year's Gunpowder Plot, for example – and gave it a twist to suit their own particular circumstances. And, inevitably, they drew on their religious faith. St Paul had told Christians in Thessalonica that they should "[b]e joyful always; pray continually; give thanks in all circumstances, for this is God's will for you in Christ Jesus" (1 Thessalonians 5:16-18), and Jesus always made a point of publicly giving thanks to God for provision of daily necessities.

> **Mayflower's Resting Place**
> Already nearing the end of her working life in 1620, the *Mayflower* was scrapped within two years of returning from America, her decaying hulk lying on the foreshore at Rotherhithe in east London. Her eventual fate is uncertain, though tradition has it that in 1624 her timbers were sold and used by Thomas Russell to extend a barn at Old Jordan, South Buckinghamshire, where a structure called the Mayflower Barn exists to this day. Evidence for this attribution is discussed by Rendell Harris in *The Finding of the Mayflower*.

> **John Robinson**
> The Pilgrims' beloved pastor never fulfilled his wish to join the members of his congregation who had journeyed to the New World, though he corresponded with them more or less until his death in 1625. He was not impressed with all he heard, rebuking them over their treatment of native tribes: "It is a thing more glorious in men's eyes than pleasing in God's, or convenient for Christians, to be a terror to poor barbarous people ... Oh! How happy a thing had it been, if you had converted some, before you killed any."

There is much we might look askance at now in what the Pilgrims did, wishing things had been done differently, or not at all. For Native Americans the coming of the *Mayflower* conjures a bitter legacy, the start of their suffering at the hands of white men. It did not have to be that way, as William

Penn later proved by holding fast to Quaker principles in Pennsylvania. The Leiden Separatists had "great hope and inward zeal ... for the propagating and advancing of the Gospel of the Kingdom of Christ in these remote parts of the world", yet too often in subsequent years, the shortcomings of sinful man were more in evidence than the better angels of our nature. Before the last of the First Comers was dead, their offspring were keeping slaves.

Sexual Equality

Biblical literalism caused many Puritans to be ahead of their time in their attitudes towards women. A typical view of the relationship between husband and wife was offered by English clergyman and theologian Thomas Gataker (1574-1654), who saw them as "together for a time as co-partners in grace here, [so that] they may reign together forever as co-heirs [with Christ] in glory hereafter". In Pilgrim's Progress, John Bunyan concluded from his reading of the Bible and the way Jesus dealt with the women he met that "women ... are highly favoured".

These missed opportunities brought doleful consequences that still haunt America.

Regret or recrimination should not overshadow the positive, however. Roughly 35 million Americans today trace their ancestry to *Mayflower* passengers, but the Pilgrims' impact reaches far beyond the physical – as trailblazers, guardians and (without quite knowing it) revolutionaries. Trailblazers who showed what was possible, helping encourage the Great Migration to New England of the 1630s. (John Winthrop's oversight of this huge undertaking drew heavily on lessons learnt from the mishaps and misadventures of the Pilgrims, and the greater knowledge of the region and its tribes to which they contributed.) Guardians, who

---

Meritocracy

Convinced that all were descended from the same original parents (Adam and Eve) and that God had not made some to be masters and others servants since all bore "the image of God" (Genesis 1:27), Puritans tended to develop egalitarian and meritocratic societies. They generally had little time for the deference expected in a hierarchical society. Hence one of the things that distinguished Quakers in a later generation was that they would not doff their caps to people who were nominally their social superiors.

---

brought *Magna Carta* and the Geneva Bible to the New World – each indispensable to the development of freedom and moulding of what became the United States. Revolutionaries, who seeded an attitude of mind which characterised not only New England, but the infant nation as a whole – birthing a freedom-loving reflex that made probable (perhaps, inevitable) the conflict which led the Thirteen Colonies to break from the mother country.

Investment

The Great Migration's success depended on funding as well as planning – an investment of £200,000 over thirteen years, equal to roughly US $40 million today (much more if calculated proportionate to GDP). Between 1630 and 1640 over 200 ships transported 14,000 settlers, including skilled workers: tanners, weavers, fishermen, chandlers, coopers, tailors, bakers, blacksmiths, butchers, carpenters, masons, merchants, leather workers, doctors and armourers. They took supplies of every kind: soap, candles, tools, clothing, shoes, furniture, cattle, horses, fodder and 10,000 gallons of beer.

Democracy was inseparable from the worldview of the Pilgrims because giving everyone access to the Scriptures was a democratic process; because allowing each

> **The American Revolution**
>
> Commentators in the 18th century noted parallels between the participants and ideals of America's Revolutionary War and England's Civil War a century earlier. Reverend William Jones wrote, "This has been a Presbyterian war from the beginning as certainly as that in 1641 [i.e. the Scottish uprising against Charles I that helped trigger civil war in England the following year]." When Cornwallis surrendered at Yorktown, all but one of the colonels in Washington's army was an elder of the Presbyterian Church. Puritans, of course, comprised not just Presbyterians but also Independents (Congregationalists), Separatists and a panoply of other sects.

"gathered community" of believers to order their own affairs militated against any form of state control and empowered individuals; because the need for each man and woman to "work out their salvation with fear and trembling" (Philippians 2:12) required choice, and choice is the enemy of dictatorship; because asserting, "We must obey God rather than men!" (Acts 5:29) meant that the hold which the mechanisms beloved of tyrants could exercise on the minds and actions of the populace was limited; and because the belief that God created mankind in His own image set none higher than another, so that logically all should be allowed an equal say.

Puritans and Separatists could not be made to fit into a world governed by Divine Right. Their habit of insisting on inconveniences like due process, the right to trial by jury, the ancient privileges of Parliament and the provisions of *Magna Carta* made them an irritant at best, a potential source of rebellion at worst. These are what made the *Mayflower Compact* such a powerful marker – not only of what was, but also of what was to come. The world owes its authors a great debt of gratitude.

> **Brother Jonathan**
>
> Up to the middle 19th century the archetype of America was not Uncle Sam (the first recorded use of which is in 1812), but Brother Jonathan. The name goes back at least to the English Civil War, when it was applied to the Puritan Roundheads, but in time it became a personification both of New England and ultimately of America. During the American Revolutionary War, British officers applied the name to their rebel opponents, recognising that supporters and enemies of the Crown were divided along similar confessional lines as in the Great Rebellion (Civil War) of the 17th century.

Afterword

"Despotism may govern without faith, but liberty cannot."

De Tocqueville

TO UPROOT YOURSELF FROM HOME, FRIENDS, FAMILY AND ALL that is familiar and comfortable to make a new life in a strange, faraway and potentially hostile place is something few would contemplate without compelling reasons. The Pilgrims were refugees twice over – first quitting England to seek asylum in the Netherlands before embarking on their epic passage to the New World just over ten years later. They crossed the North Atlantic in full knowledge of the stupendous risks, aware that there was little realistic prospect of outside help if things went wrong. It was by any standard a daunting prospect, requiring push as well as pull.

As is well known, the push was provided by religious persecution. Often, we tend to leave it at that, but it is worthwhile reflecting on the religious dimension in more detail. In a Western culture that often gives the impression of wanting to suck religion out of public life entirely, it takes an effort to put ourselves in the shoes of people for whom the Bible had as much to say about politics as about church affairs or personal devotions – an attitude that was not confined to extremists but was the view of the overwhelming majority. Since the Pilgrims and those who shared their views were so few in number, and since no-one doubted they were Protestant, the issue is why it was felt necessary to hound them at all. What was it about their views that made them so dangerous in the eyes of King James? The answer ultimately is as much political as religious, and it is as we look at the society the Pilgrims built in New England that we see the stark differences between the choices their faith led them to make and the king's alternative vision for the nation. Competing philosophies leading to different choices and distinct outcomes – something for us to take to heart today.

And in fact, religion provided the pull factor, too. The Pilgrims believed God was calling them to go to America in order to plant Christianity there. We may or may not think this conviction deluded. We may or may not think other factors played a part, too – disillusionment with life in the Netherlands, a looming prospect of renewed war between that country and imperial Spain, the negative effect of Dutch culture on their young people – but there is no reason not to take their self-professed aim at face value. These were people who had stood firm for their beliefs against all hardship, every official sanction and widespread societal condemnation. To respond to what they thought God commanded was completely consistent with all they had hitherto said and done. So, if religion was the principal motivating factor on both sides of the equation, it deserves our careful attention.

Politics in England in the early 17th century was increasingly coalescing around diametrically opposed views of church and state – eventually leading to civil war in the 1640s and the execution of King Charles I in 1649. Divine Right left no room for conscience, yet the Bible said a Christian's duty was to obey God rather than man. King James had it that kings were authors of the law, not the law of kings, whilst Scripture showed that God's law came first and man's second. The king asserted he was the rightful monarch purely by inheritance through bloodline, whereas the history of ancient Israel suggested their early kings had also required acclamation by the people. James Stuart wanted a hierarchical Church run by appointed archbishops and bishops with himself at the head – desirable both because it was easy for him to control and as it mirrored the hierarchical society he saw as the political ideal – but people like the Pilgrims saw the biblical model as one of self-governing churches with leaders chosen by the congregation. The king thought he could claim unquestioning obedience and loyalty, though the Bible was full of examples of people whom God called to take a stand against tyrants. Divine Right could not coexist with ideas like these, hence the sovereign's desire to stamp them out before the infection could spread.

On one side of the equation, then, the choice was autocracy. Now consider what the Pilgrims offered in its stead, and why. *Democracy* – because in emulation of Moses and his arrangements for ancient Israel their congregations chose their leaders and they carried that principle over into politics. *Lack of deference and hierarchy* – because human beings were equal in the way they were made (Genesis said everyone was created in the image of God) and in the way they were saved (not by any merit or activity of our own but simply because Jesus died for our sins). *Government based on the consent of the people* – because they were not only covenanted individually with God but had also covenanted together as his people, a covenant they extended from the religious sphere into the secular realm. *Freedom of conscience* – because to accept or reject Christ involved choice and this could only be meaningful if freely made. *Separation of church and state* – because they had seen how this worked in practice in the Netherlands and did not want a repeat of the suffering King James had caused by his misuse of ecclesiastical courts.

These ideas do not seem particularly radical to us now because they are common currency today, but four centuries ago none of this was obvious. Reminding ourselves what gave them birth is hugely important, the more so since a creed quite different from that of the Pilgrims has laid claim to this legacy. Ask most people where we get the idea of democracy and they will in all likelihood point to ancient Greece. Get them to reflect on liberty of speech or conscience and at a pinch they might recall Voltaire's dictum, "I disapprove of what you say, but I will defend to the death your right to say it." Lead them through the panoply of freedoms that are too often taken for granted in the West and probably they will see these as fruits of the Enlightenment. Few would trace them back to a biblical origin or ground them in a Judaeo-Christian ethic. Here lies the great value of the Pilgrims' story for us today, since if we follow unerringly where it leads, we will come upon the true source of what has (until recent years at any rate) been the bedrock of Western civilisation. Understanding this grounding – often unspoken, not always uncontested – is fundamental to making properly informed decisions about where we should now be heading.

These things matter because ideas translate into action. What we believe and hold dear determines what we will give time and preference to, what we will do and refrain from doing. It has consequences not just in terms of individual lives but also for the lives of nations, since it affects the institutions we build, the sort of education we promote and so forth. At root there is a chasm between the Bible's concept of what human beings are and how they should relate both to each other and to the world around, as compared with the vision offered by (for example) Thomas Paine's *Rights of Man* or the *Declaration of the Rights of Man and of the Citizen* promulgated by Revolutionary France in 1789. If we doubt that, we need only consider *Democracy in America*, where Alexis de Tocqueville reflected on how and why revolution in his native France so quickly collapsed into bloodshed and dictatorship whilst the American version – inspired by many of the same ideals – did not. The French nobleman concluded that a different outcome resulted largely from his fellow-countrymen's attempt to stamp out Christianity. With biblical foundations uprooted, there was little or nothing to stand in the way of The Terror and Napoleon's military adventurism.

Or mark what happened in the Pilgrims' homeland just a generation after the *Mayflower* sailed. The issues in England's civil war of the 1640s came down to tyranny or freedom – a king's claim to have unfettered power on the one hand, constitutional constraints on what the executive could do on the other. Puritans supported Parliament to a man, impelled by the same biblical worldview that caused the Pilgrims also to defy the law of the land, albeit their resistance was passive rather than violent. This Puritan reflex meant there was widespread sympathy amongst British Nonconformists a century later as American colonists took a stand against high-handed treatment by George III's government.

Time and again, we see that those who believe they have a duty to obey God rather than man and that God's law takes precedence over the dictates of the powerful are highly resistant to state attempts at coercion. Can we have genuine freedom, democracy and rule of law without the Bible? History suggests not. If remembering the Pilgrims helps us rediscover this essential truth, they will have done us a great service indeed.

Bibliography

Bayly, Christopher (ed.), *Atlas of the British Empire,* The Hamlyn Publishing Group Limited, 1989.

Bradford, William, *The History of Plymouth Plantation 1620-1647,* Houghton Mifflin Company, 1912.

Bunker, Nick, *Making haste from Babylon: The Mayflower Pilgrims and their world,* Pimlico, 2011.

Davies, Norman, *Europe: a history,* Pimlico 1997.

Hopper, Kenneth and William, *The Puritan Gift,* L. B. Tauris & Co Ltd 2009.

Johnson, Caleb, *Here shall I die ashore – Stephen Hopkins: Bermuda Castaway, Jamestown Survivor and Mayflower Pilgrim,* Xlibris Corporation 2007.

Johnson, Caleb, *The Mayflower and her passengers,* Xlibris Corporation 2006.

McEvedy, Colin, *The Penguin Atlas of Modern History (volume three),* Penguin 1986.

Mourt, *Mourt's Relation* (a.k.a. *A Relation or Journal of the Beginning and Proceedings of the English Plantation Settled at Plimouth in New England.*)

Moynahan, Brian, *If God spare my life: William Tyndale, the English Bible and Sir Thomas More – a story of martyrdom and betrayal,* Little Brown and Company 2002.

Ozment, Steven, *Protestants: the birth of a revolution,* Fontana Press 1993.

Parker, Geoffrey, *The Dutch Revolt,* Penguin 2002.

Parker, Geoffrey, *Global Crisis: war, climate change and catastrophe in the seventeenth century,* Yale University Press 2013.

Philbrick, Nathaniel, *Mayflower: a voyage to war,* Harper Perennial 2007.

Prince, Thomas, *Chronological History of New England in the Form of Annals,* Boston 1737.

Schama, Simon, *An Embarrassment of Riches: an interpretation of Dutch culture in the Golden Age,* Fontana Press 1988.

Schmidt, Gary D., *William Bradford: Plymouth's faithful pilgrim,* Eerdmans Books 1999.

Scriven, John, *Belief and the Nation,* Wilberforce Publications 2013.

Spencer, Nick, *Freedom and Order: history, politics and the English Bible,* Hodder & Stoughton 2011.

Winslow, Edward (and others), *A Relation or Journal of the Proceedings of the English Plantation Settled at Plymouth,* London, 1622.

Winslow, Edward (and others), *Good News from New England,* London 1624.

Special mention must go to the excellent website: *http://www.mayflowerhistory.com/*

Also by Philip Quenby

Redeeming a Nation
ISBN 978-1-907509-40-7

A most unique and timely book of English historical episodes and characters from a Christian perspective. Today our country is being transformed through processes such as immigration, integration of technology and economic development. Perhaps more than ever before, there is a need for this generation to find its moral and cultural bearings, in order to navigate towards social wisdom and stability. England has a history of which it can be proud.

Moses and Pharaoh
ISBN 978-1-910197-03-5

Few lands have a lineage longer or more splendid than ancient Egypt. The domain of the pharaohs has influenced nations near and far, antique and modern. The collision between the overweening pride of a venerable culture and the settled purposes of God, as described in the Book of Exodus, forms one of the climactic moments of all history. It is fundamental to understanding God's plan for his world and for each human being. Combining fascinating historical and archaeological evidence with the biblical narrative, the author highlights how Exodus applies to us today, exploring twelve broad themes against the backdrop of a turbulent period in Egyptian history.

Available from all good bookshops
and from the publisher:

onwardsandupwards.org/shop